Utterly wonderful. Emotionally attuned, s
well written, seamlessly blending theolo;
rooted in ancient practices and yet cultural
things I could say about this book, but the n

JOHN MARK COMER, author of *The Ruthless Elimination of Hurry* and founder of Practicing the Way

Self-acceptance is an uphill journey. We are told early that our value depends on our performance, grades, net worth, waist size. Fall short and feel the shame of not measuring up. How do we counterbalance this toxic tendency? Ken Shigematsu has answers worthy of our contemplation. Using strands of Scripture, neuroscience, and personal experience, Ken has woven together a tapestry of hope. Please read this book. Shame need not have the last word—not on your life.

MAX LUCADO, pastor and bestselling author

If you've ever wondered what really matters or questioned whether you are enough; if you have doubted, failed, feared, questioned, floundered, messed up, and thought yourself incapable of real change; if you have succeeded and found acclaim and yet still feel the ache of "not enough" in the pit of your stomach, then please, please, please, read this book. With clarity, humility, and courage Ken Shigematsu skillfully breaks open the goodness of love and the possibilities of discovering our own belovedness. This is the only thing that really matters. As you read this book, what is on offer is life in all its fullness and an encounter with the only power that can truly set you free to be yourself.

DANIELLE STRICKLAND, author and advocate

The universal struggle with shame is so multilayered that we need an integrated, robust approach to be free from it. Ken Shigematsu has offered us just the gift. Ken weaves theology, psychology, sociology, and more to help us become our true self. I found myself repeatedly nodding as I felt truly seen in his words. I highly recommend this book!

RICH VILLODAS, lead pastor of New Life Fellowship and author of *Good and Beautiful and Kind*

He's done it again, and then some. Ken Shigematsu's latest book is both capstone and fresh foundation—a consummation of his earlier works, a breaking of new ground. He writes with verve, insight, and humility and tells a tale at once theological, biblical, ancient, and contemporary—and so vitally important. With his skillful weaving of multiple sources and his sheer knack for storytelling, Shigematsu entertains even as he edifies. This book is necessary reading for all who wrestle with the nettlesome and perennial question, *Who am I?*

MARK BUCHANAN, author of *God Walk:*
Moving at the Speed of Your Soul

Few people could have written this deeply redemptive book. In order to write such a book, one needs to be gifted in a number of interrelated ways, which is uniquely the case with Ken Shigematsu. First, he has a wonderful capacity to see what is going on in our souls beyond what we choose to divulge. Second, Ken is also an engaging storyteller—around Vancouver many of us refer to him as the "master storyteller." Stories that touch the heart with liberating mercy. And third, Ken is not ashamed to say he feels shame. For someone of Asian descent that is not easy to do. But he has found deep grace to heal his shame; or, as I should say, Deep Grace has found him and has healed his shame. Read this book and you will find shame not only being covered but washed away in God's love. And you will find yourself, your true self, in the love of God.

DARRELL JOHNSON, retired pastor and professor, conference speaker, author, and mentor

There is a deep longing in each of us to be fully known and fully loved. But our greatest fear is that the more known we are, the less loved we'll be. Through his own vulnerable storytelling and his seamless integration of a wide array of literature from psychologists to theologians to Christian contemplatives and more, Shigematsu tenderly guides us away from toxic shame and toward true freedom. This book will lead you to drink deeply of the abundant grace found in the presence of God and through the people of God. All who are weary will find not only rest but their true and whole selves as a result.

GLENN PACKIAM, lead pastor of Rockharbor
Church and author of *The Resilient Pastor*

Through a creative blend of theology, pastoral experience, and psychological insight, Ken has written an excellent book that will help you experience healing from your shame, and a restoration of your true self. Highly recommended!

DANIEL IM, lead pastor at Beulah Alliance Church, podcaster, and author of *You Are What You Do*

There are books I read because the topic (or at least the title!) interests me. Others attract me because I know the writer. In this case both are true for me, plus the fact that I know Ken so personally and well. He writes of becoming fully the person God wants us to be so honestly and movingly out of his own life experience. *Now I Become Myself* speaks to my own longings—especially the chapters on limitations and beauty—and I believe it will speak to you.

LEIGHTON FORD, minister, evangelist, and author

While there are many resources available today about shame, *Now I Become Myself* stands out in that it is both richly Christian and widely accessible. Shigematsu's bicultural experiences in Japan (a shame/honor culture) and North America (a guilt/innocence culture) have blessed him with a deep well of insights to share. With the gentle wisdom of a pastor and the vibrant creativity of an artist, Shigematsu skillfully marshals an impressive array of illustrations from history, film, literature, music, science, pop culture, and classic spiritual writings to open our eyes to the various manifestations of shame and how to overcome it. Read this book if you want to move from the shadows of shame to the radiance of freedom and joy.

MICHELLE T. SANCHEZ, author of *Color-Courageous Discipleship* and executive minister of Make and Deepen Disciples for the Evangelical Covenant Church

We are made by God to become more than we are, made to become our true selves—an enterprise to which evil is violently opposed. To become ourselves, therefore, is the hardest task put before us. But thanks be to God, with Ken Shigematsu's *Now I Become Myself* we have a field guide of the first rank to assist us on our journey in becoming *real* human beings. With this book, we have so much more than a map for the road, for indeed our author knows well the road himself, and with his offering he is not merely telling us what to do—he is showing us how. If becoming yourself is what you long for, look no further to begin, and allow what you hold in your hands to inspire you to do the work required to become what you have not heretofore imagined.

CURT THOMPSON, MD, author of *The Soul of Shame*

This book unpacks the beautiful truth of the gospel and its power to remove the blinders of shame so we can become all that God has created us to be. Ken shines a light so we can come out of hiding, showing how the truth sets us free, and how we can experience fullness of life in Jesus.

D. J. CHUANG, author of *MultiAsian Church* and host of the Erasing Shame podcast

Shame thrives in silence and isolation. By bringing shame—and its many masks and qualities—to the fore, Shigematsu creates a space for us to examine it and ultimately set it down in favor of what is true about ourselves as God's creation whom he has called good. Filled with useful insights, practices, and stories, this book is like a mirror we can hold up against ourselves to see who we really are underneath the mask of shame.

HILLARY L. MCBRIDE, PhD, registered psychologist, podcaster, author, and speaker

Ken has written a book that is gripping both in the sense that its terrifically well-written but also in that it is spiritually arresting and soul-healing. He is deeply informed on the topic by Scripture, by wisdom, by the social sciences, and by his own open heart. In a world that often seems to be moving toward a shame/honor society, this book will foster a journey from shame to grace.

JOHN ORTBERG, founder, BecomeNew. com and author of *Soul Keeping*

Wow. Imagine you could meet with a committee consisting of a deeply empathetic friend, a wise biblical scholar, a sharp neuroscience researcher, and a wildly motivating personal coach—all of whom had the uncanny ability to read your mail, diagnose your symptoms, and offer you a path to health and flourishing. That's just what you'll get if you read *Now I Become Myself*. In a culture that is relentlessly corrosive to our identity as God's beloved, Shigematsu's book is more than timely—it's essential.

CAROLYN ARENDS, recording artist, author, and Renovaré director of education

Now I Become
MYSELF

Now I Become
MYSELF

How Deep Grace Heals Our Shame
and Restores Our True Self

KEN SHIGEMATSU

ZONDERVAN
REFLECTIVE

ZONDERVAN REFLECTIVE

Now I Become Myself
Copyright © 2023 by Ken Shigematsu

Requests for information should be addressed to:
Zondervan, *3900 Sparks Dr. SE, Grand Rapids, Michigan 49546*

Zondervan titles may be purchased in bulk for educational, business, fundraising, or sales promotional use. For information, please email SpecialMarkets@Zondervan.com.

ISBN 978-0-310-14427-4 (softcover)
ISBN 978-0-310-14429-8 (audio)
ISBN 978-0-310-14428-1 (ebook)

Lines from the poem "Now I Become Myself," by May Sarton on p. 156 in *Collected Poems, 1930–1973* (New York: Norton, 1974), used by permission of the publisher.

The welcoming prayer by Mary Mrozowski as found in *The Welcoming Prayer: Consent on the Go, a 40-Day Praxis* (West Milford, NJ: Contemplative Outreach, 2018), used with permission of the publisher.

All Scripture quotations, unless otherwise indicated, are taken from The Holy Bible, New International Version®, NIV®. Copyright © 1973, 1978, 1984, 2011 by Biblica, Inc.® Used by permission of Zondervan. All rights reserved worldwide. www.Zondervan.com. The "NIV" and "New International Version" are trademarks registered in the United States Patent and Trademark Office by Biblica, Inc.®

Scripture quotations marked ESV are taken from the ESV® Bible (The Holy Bible, English Standard Version®). Copyright © 2001 by Crossway, a publishing ministry of Good News Publishers. Used by permission. All rights reserved.

Scripture quotations marked NLT are taken from the Holy Bible, New Living Translation. © 1996, 2004, 2015 by Tyndale House Foundation. Used by permission of Tyndale House Publishers, Inc., Carol Stream, Illinois 60188. All rights reserved.

Scripture quotations marked TPT are taken from The Passion Translation®. Copyright © 2017 by BroadStreet Publishing® Group, LLC. Used by permission. All rights reserved.

Any internet addresses (websites, blogs, etc.) and telephone numbers in this book are offered as a resource. They are not intended in any way to be or imply an endorsement by Zondervan, nor does Zondervan vouch for the content of these sites and numbers for the life of this book.

All rights reserved. No part of this publication may be reproduced, stored in a retrieval system, or transmitted in any form or by any means—electronic, mechanical, photocopy, recording, or any other—except for brief quotations in printed reviews, without the prior permission of the publisher.

Cover design: Stephanie Martens
Cover image: © wbritten / Getty Images Plus
Interior design: Sara Colley

Printed in the United States of America

23 24 25 26 27 28 29 30 31 32 /TRM/ 14 13 12 11 10 9 8 7 6 5 4 3 2 1

*To Leighton Ford,
in whose presence
you feel no shame*

CONTENTS

1. THE FEAR OF NOT BEING ENOUGH 1

2. COVERED BY GRACE 17

3. ENCOUNTERING THE LOVE OF GOD 33

4. SEEING GOD'S FACE IN OTHERS 49

5. MASTERPIECE IN THE MAKING 67

6. OVERCOMING ENVY 85

7. EMBRACING OUR LIMITS 103

8. FULFILLING OUR POTENTIAL 121

9. AWAKENING TO BEAUTY 135

10. CHOOSING JOY. 147

Epilogue: Nothing Wasted. 169

Acknowledgments 181

Notes 183

Chapter 1

THE FEAR OF NOT
BEING ENOUGH

For as long as I can remember, I've had this recurring nightmare. I'm a student, facing an exam for which I am completely unprepared. It is usually in math or French, and I have forgotten to attend class or do any of the coursework. The term is almost over, and I suddenly realize that I have a big exam that I'm completely unprepared for, and I'm gripped with panic as I realize that I'm going to get a terrible mark and my grade point average will sink through the floor.

Since becoming a pastor, I've had another recurring nightmare. I'm in a church sanctuary during a worship service as the offering is being taken, and I am about to get up and preach—but I have *no idea* what to say. I frantically scratch out an outline on some scrap paper. When the offering is finished, I get up, move to the pulpit, and glance down at my notes, but to my horror, the paper is filled with indecipherable symbols: #!%?3^R*^&. As I wing it, the auditorium slowly empties as people get up and leave.

At a subconscious level, these nightmares reveal my fear of being deficient. Of not measuring up, falling flat, and losing face.

All of us struggle at some level with the feeling that we are not good enough, either in the eyes of others or in our own eyes. We might feel this when we are alone with our thoughts or in the presence of someone strikingly attractive, successful, or whose approval we crave.

When we fail or do not do as well as we had hoped, we often start to doubt our abilities. When we sense someone being distant or backing away, we may feel a tinge of rejection and wonder, "What's wrong with me?"

We can also feel self-consciousness about our bodies. When I was younger, I played a lot of basketball. During practice scrimmages or pickup games, one team would be "shirts" and the other team would be "skins" (shirtless). I'm skinny now, but I was even skinnier back then, and I would always hope and pray that I would be a "shirt" because I didn't want people to see how skinny I was.

We may feel inferior because of some dysfunction in our family, or because we think we don't have enough money, or because we've struggled with porn or some other addictive habit.

In daily circumstances, we may feel that we haven't been sufficiently present for certain people, have failed to respond to emails or messages, have neglected to keep our house or desk tidy, or haven't exercised enough or eaten well.

In the ancient world, the biblical writers described this feeling as "shame." Modern social science researchers, such as Brené Brown, also use the word "shame" to describe this sense of not being enough in our own estimation or in the eyes of someone else.

But this feeling of not being enough isn't confined to those who have failed or underachieved, those who have been abused or gone through trauma, those who have a visible disability, or those who were told as children that they were stupid, fat, ugly, or would never amount to anything.

This nagging feeling of not being quite enough is also present in those who were raised in loving families. My mom and dad were born and brought up in Japan. By Western standards, they were reserved in their expressions of affection (they didn't hug my siblings and me, nor did they ever say, "I love you"), and yet we never doubted their love.

I am so grateful for this solid foundation of love in my own life, which continues to form me to this day. But there's still a part of me that feels I only have worth if I can preach well, am a loving husband, an engaged father, or a decent athlete for my age.

This feeling of inadequacy is even present in those who are very successful by the standards of this world.

My father-in-law was one of the most successful people I have known. He served as the president of one of Japan's great, historic food companies and was highly respected for his foresight into the Japanese economy. In the year 2000, he was identified by one of Japan's leading magazines as one of the one hundred most influential people in the country who would shape the new millennium. He met with a president of the United States as part of a select group of business leaders in Japan and dined with the pope because his company helped foster the restoration of the frescoes in the Sistine Chapel. Despite being one of the outstanding business leaders of his generation, he had a nagging sense that he wasn't quite enough. He lived with a lingering insecurity that baffled me, given his accomplishments.

Michelle Obama, the brilliant and dynamic former First Lady of the United States, is a descendant of slaves and grew up in a family of modest means on the south side of Chicago. In her memoir *Becoming*, she says that when she was in kindergarten, she remembers wondering, "Am I good enough?" As she entered high school, college, and then law school, she continued to wonder, "Am I good enough?" When she worked in the corporate world and then in the nonprofit arena, she still wondered, "Am I good enough?"

And even after becoming First Lady of the United States, she says, "I have become by certain measures a person of power, and yet there are moments still when I feel insecure or unheard."[1] After all her extraordinary achievements, she still wonders, *Am I good enough?*

Similarly, Whitney Houston, the most-awarded female recording artist of all time, struggled with insecurity and anxiety about measuring up. When her friend Kevin Costner asked her to costar in *The Bodyguard*, she had her doubts. On her first day on the set, after her hair and makeup were ready, he said, "Whitney was scared. Arguably, the biggest pop star in the world wasn't sure if she was good enough. She didn't think she looked right. There were a thousand things that seemed wrong to her. I held her hand and told her that she looked beautiful . . . but I could still feel the doubt."

Whitney asked for twenty minutes to collect herself, and then she came to the set. After only four lines, they had to stop. Costner took her back to the dressing room so she could see herself in the mirror. He recounted the scene:

> She gasped. All of the makeup . . . [was] streaking down her face and she was devastated. She didn't feel like the makeup we put on her was enough so she'd wiped it off

and put on [her own]. It was much thicker and the hot lights had melted it! She asked if anyone had seen . . . [and] I said I didn't think so. . . . The Whitney I knew, despite her success and worldwide fame, still wondered, *"Am I good enough? Am I pretty enough? Will they like me?"*[2]

No matter how accomplished we might become, we will all continue to feel self-doubt. But can this feeling that we are not enough ever be helpful?

As philosophers, preachers, and psychologists have long pointed out, guilt—the feeling that we have *done* something wrong—can be helpful in changing negative behaviors.

Guilt can act like a light on the dashboard of our car, indicating that something is wrong with the engine and prompting us to take corrective action.

But guilt can also be unhealthy. False guilt from an overly scrupulous conscience or unresolved guilt will eat up our insides and may cause physical symptoms, such as back pain and headaches.[3]

The Social Utility of Shame

Can shame ever be healthy?

While many people today think that any feeling of shame is always toxic, there are situations when social shame can be healthy.

For example, the apostle Paul uses shame out of loving, pastoral concern to exhort people at the church in Corinth to treat each other with more decency (1 Corinthians 6:5).

And in his second letter to the Corinthians, Paul writes: "For the kind of sorrow God wants us to experience leads us away from sin and results in salvation" (2 Corinthians 7:10 NLT).

Just as there is a kind of "godly sorrow" that ultimately leads to life, there is a "godly shame" that can reveal how we are acting wrongly or causing hurt in the world. This feeling of shame can turn us toward God and help us align ourselves with his good purposes for us and for the larger world.

Those who do not experience this kind of redemptive shame are often seen as lacking in conscience or sociopathic.

Through the prophet Jeremiah, God asks: "Are they ashamed of their detestable conduct? No, they have no shame at all; they do not even know how to blush" (Jeremiah 6:15).

None of us want to be people who are shameless or incapable of blushing.

Some shame can be redemptive. The possibility of facing shame can curb our tendency to do something wrong, because we don't want to experience a loss of social standing and connection with others.

In my country of origin, Japan, a politician might feel guilt at accepting a bribe, but he would feel shame if he were caught and exposed in the press. While we may feel guilt after breaking a moral code, we feel shame when we do something wrong and then it is exposed to others in a social context. Throughout Asia and most of the world, with the exception of the post-Enlightenment West, shame is an important social emotion that is used to signal that someone has lost standing in the community.[4]

In the age of social media, our lives are more exposed than ever before. Though shame has been suppressed in the *laissez-faire* culture of the post-Enlightenment West, it is making a comeback because we are all afraid of doing anything that might threaten our connection to a group that is important to us.[5]

As psychologist Dr. Hillary McBride points out, belonging is central to our identity and survival, so our central nervous system alerts us to anything that might jeopardize our belonging by telling us, in effect: "Do you see how they are looking at you? *Stop* what you're doing now, because that look is threatening your belonging in the tribe."[6]

The Costs of Toxic Shame

But when we experience shame repeatedly, we may begin to generalize the shame toward *ourselves* rather than attaching it to our behavior. Rather than thinking, "I *did* something bad," we begin to believe, "I *am* bad." We move from a *temporary* experience of shame as a *state* to shame as a personal *trait*.

While a temporary *state* of shame can inspire life change and may have a social benefit, my focus in this book is to help us overcome our unhealthy *trait* shame—the feeling that we are fundamentally flawed and therefore unworthy.[7]

Trait shame is toxic and needs to be uprooted and eradicated because it drives us for the wrong reasons.

The pop star Madonna, who has constantly reinvented herself, once said, "I am driven to succeed out of the fear of feeling mediocre and uninteresting."[8]

Similarly, Arnold Schwarzenegger, an actor and former governor of California, said, "I feel driven to achieve because growing up I never felt good enough, or smart enough, or strong enough."[9]

When Barack Obama reflected on his motives for running for president, he wondered, "Was I trying to prove myself worthy to a father who had abandoned me, live up to my mother's starry-eyed expectations for her only son, resolve any self-doubt that remained of being born a child of mixed race?"[10] His wife, Michelle, observed that it was like he had a hole he needed to fill, which at times caused him to work to the point of exhaustion.

Shame not only exists in impoverished, crime-ridden, drug-infested parts of the inner city but also in legislative halls, corner offices of corporate skyscrapers, and the ivory towers of academic and religious institutions with those who are driven to prove something.

Shame can either drive us to inflate ourselves and "go big" or cause us to shrink back, making us feel smaller and more hesitant.

When I was in sixth grade, I went to a roller-skating rink with some of my buddies. We watched a girl with long, wavy blonde hair pivot to a backwards skate effortlessly, then jump and twirl like a figure skater. She was the goddess of the place. We were all attracted to her, but my friends were too afraid to ask her to "couples skate" (hold hands while skating to a romantic song). I was pretty confident as a sixth grader—in fact, that was probably my all-time social peak!—so I decided to impress my friends. As I skated up to her, I found myself looking *up* at her and felt my confidence

> *Shame can either drive us to inflate ourselves and "go big" or cause us to shrink back, making us feel smaller and more hesitant.*

ebbing away. "Do you want to couples skate with me?" I asked. She looked me up and down, then said, "No." Though I can look back now and chuckle, my sixth-grade heart was crushed.

This experience made me more inhibited around girls, and as a teenager I was afraid to ask them out on dates.

When we feel unlovable or unworthy, the nerve endings in our bodies pull our eyes and mouths down. Quite literally, our bodies say, "Disengage, disconnect, you're going to get rejected. It's too painful." To thrive, we need connection with others. When shame pulls us away from others, it becomes more and more difficult for us to stay connected and to receive and offer love.

Shame also inhibits us from speaking up for ourselves or speaking out on behalf of someone else. Shame can prevent us from launching a new venture or embarking on a creative project because we are paralyzed by the fear that we will look foolish or feel humiliated.

While I have lived most of my life in North America, I was born in Japan and travel back to visit on a regular basis. Japan is a shame-and-honor society, so people assess their own self-worth according to how they are seen by others based on their family of origin, the school they attended, the company they work for, or their role in society. While the pressure to be respectable and successful spawns impressive productivity in Japan, it can also be oppressive.

At the time of this writing, according to government estimates, more than a million people have opted out of society through a phenomenon called *hikikomori* where young people refuse to go to school and adults renounce work and literally spend their entire existence in their bedrooms. They feel they can't compete in the system, so out of fear of being seen as a failure, they cocoon themselves in the anonymity of their rooms.[11]

While most of our experiences are not as extreme, shame does cause us to hold back in ways that can lead to regret.

In a *New York Times* essay, Roger Cohen writes: "It seems, as we grow older, that we are haunted less by what we have done than by what we failed to do, whether through lack of courage, or inattention, or insufficient readiness to cast caution to the winds. The impossible love abandoned, the gesture unmade, the heedless voyage untaken . . ."[12]

The feeling of shame can also cause us to act in a shameless manner. As a pastor, I have observed that when someone experiences sexual abuse as a child, they lose sight of their inestimable value, experience a great deal of self-loathing and shame, and can become promiscuous because they feel like "damaged goods" with nothing of value to protect.

In Dostoyevsky's novel *Crime and Punishment*, Sonya, the saintly daughter of a destitute, drunkard father, is put down by someone in her household, who tells her she is not contributing enough to the household. Shamed, she leaves the house, sells her body on the street as a prostitute, then comes home and lays rubles on the kitchen table.[13]

Shame also causes us to shame others. A lot of the toxicity of our public discourse today is caused by the shame that people carry from their past experiences. Hurt people hurt others. Shamed people shame others. We pass on what we have received.

In *The World Is Flat*, the *New York Times* columnist Thomas Friedman writes:

It has always been my view that terrorism is not spawned by the poverty of money; it is spawned by the poverty of dignity. Humiliation is the most underestimated force in international relations and in human relations. It is when people or nations are humiliated that they really lash out and engage in extreme violence.

When you take the economic and political backwardness of much of the Arab-Muslim world today, add its past grandeur and self-images of religious superiority, and combine it with the discrimination and alienation that these Arab-Muslim males face when they leave home and move to Europe, or when they grow up in Europe, you have one powerful cocktail of rage.[14]

Friedman cites his friend, the Egyptian playwright Ali Salem: "[The 911 hijackers] are walking the streets of life, searching for tall buildings—for towers to bring down, because they are not able to be tall like them."

Shame can cause us to envy others and then seek to cut them down to make ourselves feel taller or to belittle them to make ourselves seem larger.[15]

Overcoming Unhealthy Shame

What is the answer to shame?

Many of us believe that if we can only accomplish something special, we will overcome our shame and finally begin to feel that we are enough.

While developing competence is good and healthy, my father-in-law's experience of great success coupled with deep insecurity suggests that being good at something won't necessarily help us feel deep down inside that we are enough.

Not long after Ashton Eaton received his second gold decathlon medal at the 2016 Summer Olympics in Rio de Janeiro, I wondered if he felt that his spectacular athletic achievements had made him feel like he was "enough."

"Have you seen the movie *Cool Runnings*?" I asked on a Skype call. *Cool Runnings* is loosely based on the true story of Jamaica's attempt to field its first bobsledding team for the 1988 Calgary Winter Olympic Games.

"Sure," he said.

"You know the scene when the coach walks into the room and sees his star bobsledder, Darius, studying the bobsled course?" In this scene, Darius feels the weight of the world on his shoulders because he believes that if he can only win an Olympic gold medal, people will finally see him as successful and respect him. But the coach, who has won two gold medals himself, walks over to Darius and says, "If you're not enough without the gold medal, you won't be enough with it."

Ashton remembered this scene and said without hesitation, "The coach is absolutely right! If you're not enough without the gold medal, you won't be enough with it."

He paused thoughtfully, then continued, "After winning my first gold medal in London, it felt great, but after a while I looked down at the medal and thought it's *just* a medallion. The great value of the Olympics wasn't the medal, but that it inspired me to do my best."

For Ashton, though winning a gold medal was a great honor,

it was like a cherry on top of the sundae—a sweet extra, but it didn't make him feel like *he* was enough.

Whatever "gold medal" we might be trying to attain, it won't be enough to help us feel that *we* are enough. Though we may feel a wonderful sense of elation in the moment of an achievement, it won't fill the Swiss Cheese holes inside us.[16]

Though we may feel a wonderful sense of elation in the moment of an achievement, it won't fill the Swiss Cheese holes inside us.

This restless feeling of not being enough isn't going to go away after you graduate, after you get your first job, as soon as you find someone to love, or when you receive the gift of someone else's unconditional love. These will be amazing moments, but none of them will give you an abiding sense that *you* are enough.

We will only know that we are *enough* when we experience the deep grace of God, which covers our shame, makes us whole, and calls forth our true self.

Prayer Exercise

———◇———

I hope and pray that through this book you will encounter God deeply.

To help you create space in your life to draw close to Jesus and deepen your felt experience of God's love for you, I will conclude each chapter with a prayer exercise intended to nurture your relationship with the God who formed you in love and created you in beauty, full of grace and glory.

I seek to create this space in my own life each morning by setting aside about twenty minutes for silent, meditative prayer. I begin by breathing in deeply through my nose and exhaling slowly through my nose.

The biblical Hebrew word for "breath" and "spirit" are the same, so as I breathe in, I am conscious that I am breathing in the very breath (Spirit) of God. As I breathe in, I pray a simple phrase like, "Fill me with your Spirit, Lord." Or, I simply say the word "love" as a reminder that God's nature is love. When my mind wanders or I feel restless, I pray the phrase or the word again to turn my attention back to the Lord.

As I sit in silence, emotions—such as anxiety, envy, anger, or shame—may surface. I offer these emotions up to God and experience purging and cleansing. Though these feelings may return, I offer them up to God again and experience new freedom and rest more fully in God's peace and joy.

Take a few moments now to sit and breathe in the breath (Spirit) of God. Invite God to fill you with his Spirit, using a sacred word such as love, peace, or joy to affirm the nature of God in your life.

Rest peacefully with your eyes closed, breathing deeply through your nose, until you are ready to open your eyes and move into the rest of your day.

Reflection

The peace of God, which transcends all understanding, will guard your hearts and your minds in Christ Jesus. (Philippians 4:7)

Study Guide Questions

1. Why do you think that even very successful, accomplished people fear not being enough?
2. Take a moment to reflect on an area in your life where you feel like you are not enough.
3. Have you ever experienced healthy shame? How has this experience been beneficial in your life?
4. Have you (or someone you know) ever experienced toxic shame? How has unhealthy shame been destructive in your life (or the life of someone you know)?
5. How can we overcome harmful shame?

Chapter 2

COVERED BY GRACE

*There is only one problem on which all my existence,
my peace and my happiness depend: to discover myself
in discovering God. If I find Him, I will find myself,
and if I find my true self I will find Him.*
—THOMAS MERTON[1]

When I was in junior high, I wanted to impress my friend Charlie, who was a popular football player at our school, so I invited him to Kmart so I could show him just how easy it was to shoplift. I was wearing a Vancouver Canucks hockey jacket with holes in the liner of the pockets, and I would place the things I stole between the outer shell and inner lining of the jacket. Charlie and I walked over to the sporting goods section, and I slid a baseball batting glove into my pocket. I clasped a small black rubber ball in my fist and shoved it into the right front pocket of my jeans. In my fervor, I started stealing things that I didn't even want (like earrings) just to show off.

As we walked out of the store together, a man walked up behind me, tapped me on the shoulder, and said, "I am a store detective, come with me." Charlie turned his head, looked at me with wide-eyed astonishment, and said, "I gotta go."

The detective called my parents, who came to the store to pick me up and drove me home. As we entered my room, my dad told me in Japanese to kneel. Kneeling in the traditional Asian style was painful—then, as now, I was not flexible. My parents knelt next to me, and my mom was crying. "You have brought shame on us and our whole family," my dad said, and then he struck me—a common practice among many immigrant families at that time. While this was not the first time I had received his physical discipline, I had never felt his anger with such intensity.

Later that night, I stood at the top of the stairs in our house. With a painful feeling of regret and shame, I resolved that I would never again do anything that would bring so much pain to my parents. I knew I needed to take a new direction.

State Shame versus Trait Shame

The temporary *state* of feeling shame when we realize that we have lost standing in someone's eyes because we have done something wrong can be redemptive. As the theologian Lewis Smedes writes, "A healthy sense of shame is perhaps the surest sign of our divine origin and our human dignity. When we feel this sense of shame, we are feeling a nudge from our true selves."[2]

But feeling shame as a more permanent *trait*—a sense that we are fundamentally flawed and are unworthy and unlovable—is toxic and destructive.

Healthy shame can function like a proximity sensor on a car, signaling that we have veered off in the wrong direction so we can steer back toward our divine origin. In the beginning we were made in the image of God, and before "original sin" we experienced original glory.

If shame tells us that we are not living the way we were designed to live, then before sin came into the world, shame was not an emotion human beings experienced. According to Genesis, Adam and Even existed in the garden of Eden naked and *without shame.* They lived not only physically naked in each other's presence, but they were also psychologically and spiritually open and free with each other—a condition we've yearned for ever since.

But then sin and shame entered their story.

The very phrasing that Adam and Eve were both naked and felt no shame suggests that this emotion was about to enter their world. The biblical author could have written, "they were naked and happy," or "they were naked and at home with themselves and each other."[3]

Then Satan enters the garden of Eden and approaches Eve and Adam in the form of a serpent. When we hear the word "serpent," we might imagine a hideous creature slithering on its belly. But according to some biblical scholars, before the serpent was cursed, it may well have been the most dazzlingly beautiful creature in the garden.

Scripture tells us that Satan was once an angel of light, but one who apparently didn't feel like he was enough, so he aspired to be equal to God. This one who feels like he's not enough approaches Adam and Eve and insinuates that they are not enough either. He whispers, "You could be so much *more* if you eat of the Tree of Knowledge of Good and Evil. You will be just like God, knowing good from evil. You will be fulfilled and free!"

The serpent suggests that by forbidding them to eat from the Tree of Knowledge of Good and Evil, God doesn't have their best interests at heart—and literally and figuratively, Adam and Eve bite.

But do they become like God? Fulfilled and free? A better version of themselves?

No—immediately, they sense that something has been taken from them, and they experience a feeling they have never known before: shame. Their instinct is to hide. So they reach for fig leaves to cover themselves (Genesis 3:7).

> *Even as we are turning away, we are longing to experience connection and belonging, to find someone who, despite our shame, will love us and say, "I am here, and I am not going anywhere."*

When we turn away from our creator—the source of all beauty, love, and joy—instead of feeling that we are *more*, we feel that we are *less*. And even as we are turning away, we are longing to experience connection and belonging, to find someone who, despite our shame, will love us and say, "I am here, and I am not going anywhere."

Covering Ourselves

Like Adam and Eve, shame makes us feel vulnerable and exposed, and so we avert our gaze, looking down and away, or curl in on ourselves, making ourselves small. When we feel this way—whether at a conscious or unconscious level—we frantically try to do something to cover ourselves so we don't have to feel the pain of our shame.

Some of us may overwork as a way of covering our sense of deficiency. While I was in my twenties, I worked in the corporate world of Tokyo. My workday went from seven in the morning until just after eleven at night (including the commute time). In the shame and honor culture of Japan, "seven-eleven" men work long hours not only out of loyalty to the company but also to be *seen* by others as dutiful and hard-working.

Some of us might use sports as a way to cover ourselves. Growing up, I loved sports, especially informal games of hockey or football in the cul-de-sac in front of our home. But during high school, I began forming my identity around sports. I began to play sports as a way to earn respect and to impress girls who would otherwise not notice me.

Others might pursue knowledge and education as a kind of covering, a fig leaf to mask the nagging sense of not being enough. I have a brilliant and well-educated friend who has earned degrees from several prestigious schools and is a widely respected leader in his field. But in junior high, he was bullied because he wasn't athletic, and sports were valued above all else. In the schoolyard, he hid from his peers and soothed himself by silently repeating, "I'm smarter than you. I'm smarter than you. I'm smarter than you."

We can also use our ministry involvements to cover over our sense of inadequacy. Though I would love to say I have always engaged in my pastoral ministry solely for the glory of God and the good of others, if I am honest, I have to admit that a part of me has wanted to succeed in my vocation as a way to prove my worthiness.

We can also become religiously compulsive and obsessively conscientious as a way of masking our feelings of not being enough. Or we might cultivate a sculpted body, curate our image through social media, or try to raise accomplished children to cover up our inner shame.

All these psychological fig leaves of being more athletic or musical, smarter or better educated, thinner or beefier, higher on the ladder of our profession, amassing money or travel experiences, or being morally upright may make us feel temporarily better, but none of them will bring us the lasting, confident contentment we are seeking.

Trappist monk Thomas Merton observed that we try to clothe our invisible, nonexistent self in an attempt to make our invisible self more objectively real.[4] We wrap achievements, novel experiences, pleasures, and material possessions around ourselves like bandages, believing that these coverings will make our invisible selves more visible.[5]

Merton described this self that we are trying to create by what we do, have, or accomplish as our *false self*.[6]

The False Self

Living for achievement, approval, pleasure, and material security will ultimately fail to cover and protect us. All these coverings are mere fig leaves that provide a very temporary and flimsy garment.

I have a friend who is a gifted actor, who can step into a variety of personas not only on a movie set but also in real-life interviews and social situations. He can play a brash, über-confident man or a deferential and solicitous one, a charming flirt or a shy and nervous misfit. But when we project a false self, the "self" that others love is not really us.

Furthermore, when we live from our constructed false self, we cannot truly experience the love of God, for as Thomas Merton contends, God does not know (and therefore cannot love) our false self. Merton goes on to say that to be unknown by God gives us way too much privacy![7]

Coming Home to Our True Self

So how do we return to our true self? How do we recover our primal innocence of being "naked and without shame" before God? How can we exhibit the best qualities of a healthy and free child who has not yet learned to wear the cumbersome raincoat of shame, which repels the grace of God?[8]

> *How can we become who we were before the world told us who we had to be?*

In the words of a friend, how can "we become who we were before the world told us who we had to be"? How can we become more vulnerable and open, living from the deep center of our true selves rather than a projected image that will impress others or ourselves?

Where we can say with the poet May Sarton:

Now I become myself.

It's taken Time, many years and places;
I have been dissolved and shaken,
Worn other people's faces . . .

Now I become myself.[9]

How can we begin to live from our true self so we can truly experience the love of God, which will cover us with a lasting garment that protects us from the storms of life?

When we realize we have lost our keys, wallet, or something precious or important, we retrace our steps to the place we last remember having the lost item. We have all lost the innocent sense of being naked and unashamed, uninhibited and free, living from our deep center, our true self. So let us go back to where we last experienced that sense of uncovered vulnerability.

At the beginning of the biblical story, humans walked with God without shame in Eden in the cool of the day, enjoying true intimacy with the Creator. We, too, can overcome our sense of shame as we walk with God and enjoy intimacy with our Maker.

When the light of God's love shines into our lives, the diamond of our true self will be illuminated, and we will grow more beautiful and vulnerable, open and free. As we live in the light of this divine love, we will be freed of the shame that binds us.

Our deepest happiness will not come from pursuing achievement, pleasure, or material security, but from knowing and living in divine love. This love isn't something we achieve but is a gift that we receive. It is not something we can create; it is conferred on us by another.

Looking for the One Who Is Looking for Us

After Adam and Eve turn away from God and hide in the bushes, God calls out for them, asking, "Where are you?" (Genesis 3:9).

While some people may think that God is scolding or rebuking Adam and Eve, as we see in what follows, the purpose of this question is to restore connection and intimacy with them. When Adam and Eve turn away from God in the garden, they lose a glorious kind of spiritual clothing. Realizing they are naked, they sew fig leaves together as makeshift clothes for themselves.

We have a fig tree in our backyard and based on my inadvertent contact with its leaves while picking figs, I can assure you that sewing fig leaves would not make for comfortable or durable clothes. The fig leaves made my skin sticky and itchy, and I broke out in a rash.

Despite Adam and Eve's choice to separate from their maker, God, in his merciful love for them, calls out, "Where are you?" Then he makes "garments of skin for Adam and his wife and clothed them" (Genesis 3:21). The Franciscan priest Richard Rohr describes God in this moment as a nurturing seamstress, who sews them garments that are much more durable than fig leaves.[10]

By covering them, God warms them both physically and metaphysically. As biblical scholar Walter Brueggemann says, "God does for the couple what they could not do for themselves. They cannot deal with their shame, but God can, will, and does."[11]

To get those animal skins, God would have had to sacrifice an animal. Though we don't see the actual sacrifice in the narrative, it is the first death in the creation story. We don't know what kind of animal was sacrificed, but this implied sacrifice was a foreshadowing of the great sacrifice that God would make on our behalf. Millennia later, God became a human being and was given the name Jesus, which means savior. According to

Scripture, when Jesus was about thirty-three, after living a sinless life, he offered himself as the Lamb of God who takes away the sin and shame of the world.

His death by crucifixion was the ultimate shaming. After he was stripped naked, savagely beaten, and people spat in his face, a mock crown of thorns was placed on his head. Then he was nailed to a cross completely naked (not even a loin cloth), and his body most likely hung a few inches—not feet—above the ground, in full public view.

On the cross, Jesus not only atoned for our sin but also absorbed our shame. In Hebrews 12:2 we read that Jesus "endured the cross, scorning its shame." He bore our shame so we no longer need to carry it. Hebrews also tells us that the character of God "is the same yesterday and today and forever" (Hebrews 13:8). The unchanging God of the universe, who sought out Adam and Eve in the garden, made clothes for them, and restored them to relationship, continues to seek you and me.

As psychiatrist and author Curt Thompson says, "We are looking for someone who is looking for us."[12]

Being Seen and Loved

As I mentioned earlier, I was born in Japan. Because Japan is a shame-and-honor society, a Japanese person experiences shame when they fail to behave in a manner that is considered appropriate by others. What's more, a shameful act committed by one person brings shame to the entire family.

One way this shame can be removed is for someone in the family to commit hara-kiri (*seppuku*), which is a form of ritual suicide. Unlike the Western concept of suicide, where death is seen as an escape from life's pain or problems, hara-kiri demonstrates a person's willingness to assume full responsibility for the shame and to make the ultimate sacrifice to remove the shame that has fallen on his or her family and loved ones. To be clear, I am not encouraging death by suicide, but in a shame-and-honor society this voluntary offering of one's life is seen as a loving, ennobling act that erases shame, restores honor, and heals relationships.

Because of God's great love for us, Jesus willingly bore the full weight of our shame by being shamed on the cross so we would no longer have to hobble beneath its weight. When we receive this gift of having our shame erased by God in Christ, we are completely freed of shame before God, which enables us to live with less shame in our own eyes and before others.

Just as God clothes Adam and Eve with animal skins to cover their nakedness, he adorns us with gleaming garments of glory and honor (Zechariah 3:1–5, Revelation 3:5, Psalm 8:5). When we are seen, loved, and covered by God, we blossom into our best, most beautiful selves—just like a cherry tree in the first warm days of spring.

When we are seen and loved by God, our soul emerges from the safe cover of the bushes, where it has been hiding like a wild animal in the forest, and we encounter our true self. When we live from our true self, we can connect more fully with God, ourselves, and others.

I know an upstanding and committed Christian who is truly respected for his integrity. Though he grew up in a conservative Christian home and his parents never drank a drop of alcohol, my friend occasionally enjoys a glass of wine with dinner or a beer with a friend.

One night, he was downtown with a buddy, and they had a few beers at a bar.

They eventually left, but as they were walking past another bar, his friend said, "How about another beer?"

"Sure," my friend replied.

"I don't remember what happened next," he told me. "But my next memory, I'm lying on my back on a sidewalk in a drug-infested part of town, and my friend is trying to prevent someone else from beating me up. My friend pulls me onto a bus, and I end up vomiting. The bus driver pulls over and says, 'You need to get out.' The next thing I remember I'm lying in a hospital bed, hooked up to a machine, and my wife is looking at me."

Sometime thereafter, he felt compelled to share his story with two trusted friends. Overcome by shame, he was unable to speak at first, but after considerable silence, stammering, and with tears in his eyes, he recounted the incident.

His friends wept with him, prayed for him, and offered what felt like a visceral wave of love, without conditions.

Shame had reared its ferocious head, but their love proved stronger yet, breaking the power of shame and freeing him from his heavy burden.

Being Restored to Honor

In Luke 15, Jesus tells a story about a son who asked his father for his share of the inheritance. In his Middle Eastern culture, this would have been tantamount to saying, "Dad, I wish you were dead."

In this society, his father's wealth would have been directly tied to his land. Selling part of the property to cash out the share of his son's inheritance meant that some of his employees would have been forced out of work. The son would have been hated by those workers.

After receiving his inheritance, the young man goes to the Vegas of his world and blows all his money on alcohol, drugs, and prostitutes. He eventually goes hungry and ends up taking a job feeding pigs, which in his culture would have been equivalent to selling drugs on the street, but for a pittance.

In his shame-and-honor society, he has completely lost face.

Finally, desperate and miserable, he decides to return home, but he realizes that he's no longer worthy to be called his father's son. So while making the long trek home on foot, he rehearses a speech in which he'll ask his father to make him one of his hired servants.

The news of the son's return most likely reached his home village long before he arrived. In the efficient social-media network of word-of-mouth gossip in the ancient Near East, people probably would have been talking and placing bets about when the son would finally arrive home. People would have hated him, and so they would have gathered on the edge of the village to humiliate him by hurling insults and throwing things at him.

Worried that the angry villagers might hurt his son, the father scans the horizon, anticipating his homecoming and wanting to reach him first. When he sees his son as a speck in the distance, he begins to sprint toward him, lifting the ends of his robe and revealing parts of his legs—extremely shameful behavior for a grown man in the culture of his day.

The father reaches his son, embraces him, and before his son can begin his speech about not being worthy to be called his father's son, his father shouts to a servant, "Get the best new set of clothes for him and a ring for his finger." According to Dr. Kenneth Bailey, one of the world's foremost scholars of Jesus's parables, the father takes off his own robe and puts it on his son.[13] Then he takes off his own ring and puts it on his son's finger. Finally, he orders a big feast. Having been showered by love and acceptance from the father, who has status in the village, the son's shame is healed, and everyone must now accept him.

The father takes the son's shame upon himself so his son's honor can be restored.

He removes his own clothes so his son can be clothed.

This is what God has done for you in Christ. He has taken on your shame so you can live with honor. He has clothed you with his robe so you are covered by grace.

Prayer Exercise

———◇———

Breathe deeply in and out of your nose to help you relax and re-center.

As you reflect on this story in prayerful silence, let something that makes you feel ashamed rise to the surface—some part of your life where you don't feel like you are enough, something about yourself you do not like or perhaps even hate.

Now imagine that Jesus, like the father in this parable, is running toward you. Feel his embrace. Imagine him covering you with his robe and placing his ring on your finger. Listen to him declare that he wants to host a feast in your honor. Now invite him to speak words of love, affection, and blessing over you.

Reflection

At the core of shame is the fear of being unlovable and rejected, but in God's loving presence, you are seen and known, accepted and loved—for the one you are looking for is running toward you.

Study Guide Questions

1. When have you experienced a healthy sense of *state* shame? When have you experienced destructive *trait* shame?

2. What are some "fig leaves" you reach for to cover your true self? When we hide behind our "false self," why can't we experience the love of God?

3. What are some of the implications of Jesus bearing our shame (Hebrews 12:2)?

4. How does God restore our honor so we can come home to our true self?

Chapter 3

ENCOUNTERING THE LOVE OF GOD

Then you will be empowered to discover what every holy one experiences—the great magnitude of the astonishing love of Christ in all its dimensions. How deeply intimate and far-reaching is his love! How enduring and inclusive it is! Endless love beyond measurement that transcends our understanding—this extravagant love pours into you until you are filled to overflowing with the fullness of God!
—EPHESIANS 3:18–19 TPT

When my four siblings and I were just starting out in our careers, I was on a path that would eventually lead to vocational Christian ministry. My older sister was just beginning a career in television. My brother was on the road to becoming a playwright. Another sister was preparing to become a professor—a vocation that at times would embroil her in controversy. My youngest sister was studying to become a high school teacher and guidance counselor, and she observed,

"We've all had the confidence to do things we've really wanted to, even if it meant taking a risk and possible failure, because we've always known that no matter what, Mom and Dad would love us unconditionally and let us come back home if we ever needed a place to stay!"

From the research of John Bowlby, the renowned twentieth-century British psychologist and psychiatrist, and Mary Main, a professor at the University of California at Berkeley, we know that children who are nurtured and have a warm connection with a parent or a significant caregiving adult, such as a grandparent, teacher, or important babysitter, experience what is described as "secure attachment."[1] From this place of secure attachment, these children are more likely to be able to form healthy attachments with others across their lifetime and also to take healthy risks. Secure attachment helps people face new experiences with curiosity rather than fear.

Research also shows that children who grow up with cold, distant, and critical relationships and never experience secure attachments with a parent or significant adult are more likely to experience what is described as "insecure attachment." They tend to become anxious and fearful and are less likely to form healthy attachments or pursue life-giving adventure.

The data also demonstrate that a person's attachment patterns can change from insecure to secure, but this will not occur without a significant influence from an outside relationship or a dramatic shift in life circumstances.[2]

For example, let's say a sensitive eight-year-old boy lives in a family where emotions aren't acknowledged or valued, and he's not attached closely to his parents, but he has a second-grade teacher who sees and "gets" him. His capacity for attachment can grow from insecure to secure.

Or let's say a teenager is living in the wake of her mother's anxiety at home, but she has a coach or a youth group leader who asks her questions about her life. As a result, this teenager may begin to feel seen and move from a place of insecurity to security, where she can develop healthy attachments to others and pursue risks worth taking.[3]

Or a woman, who grew up with a father who was not present to her and was involved in several affairs might become wary of men and shut down her longing for connection. But then she finds herself in a relationship with someone who is open and loving, and as he slowly invites her to take the risk of trust, she shifts from a place of insecure attachment to one of more secure attachment.[4]

> *From the womb to the tomb, our lives can be profoundly transformed and made more whole through connection and love.*

For a long time, it was widely believed that a person needed to experience secure attachment as an infant or a very young child, or they would never be able to form secure attachments as an adult. While it is critically important for a young child to experience a deep sense of love and security, we now know that it's never too late. From the womb to the tomb, our lives can be profoundly transformed and made more whole through connection and love.[5]

When we feel seen, known, and loved by another human being, psychiatrist and author Curt Thompson explains that the left and right hemispheres of our brain connect, new neural networks form, and we experience a greater level of integration and wholeness.[6]

Attached to God

The most powerful and transformative experience of being known and loved comes from our relationship with our Creator.

When we sense not just on an intellectual level but also in a deeply personal way that we are seen, known, and loved by our Maker, we live with more joy and peace. Because we will experience a greater sense of security, we will be able to form healthier relationships and live with more courage and boldness.

During my early teen years, my two overriding goals in life were to have fun and to be part of the popular "in" group. As I shared in the introduction, I was terrified of rejection throughout those years, particularly in romantic pursuits. In my high school, it was cool to engage in risky, rebellious behavior, and so to impress my peers and gain their acceptance (as I shared in chapter 2), I started shoplifting. I also had a friend who worked at a local car repair shop, and we used to "borrow" the cars he was repairing and take them joyriding. Then I started using drugs and even got into small-time dealing.

My dad, who was a traditional Japanese person of impeccable integrity, confronted me and told me I had brought shame on the family. Then he took me on a "field trip" to a local prison and wryly said, "I just wanted you to see your future home. You'll be getting free room and board thanks to my tax dollars."

Scaring me straight didn't work when I was fourteen, and so my father, who had recently become a follower of Jesus, took me to a Christian youth conference. On the last day of the conference, the speaker asked, "If you were to die tonight, would you know for certain that you were going to heaven?" Although I wasn't thinking much about death as an adolescent, I remember hanging my head pensively and thinking, *I am far from God.*

The speaker then explained that God loved us, became a human being in Jesus Christ, and died on a cross as a sacrifice for our sins so we could experience forgiveness and be given a clean slate. While I didn't have a literal vision, when I heard these words, I felt like the light of God's love was shining down on me.

I had an intuitive sense that offering my life up to the source of this love would cost me my place in the popular group, but I also felt that embracing the love and forgiveness of God was the most precious gift I could receive, an offer too good to pass up. In that moment, I felt acute shame for my sins and shortcomings, but I had an even greater sense of God's love washing over me.

That first burst of understanding that God loved *me* slowly began to change how I saw myself. Over time, I came to feel that if God loved me, I could and should accept and love myself. My life did not change overnight, but looking back, I can see that this was a significant turning point for me.

Although my felt sense of God's love has waned and swelled over the years, my life has been forever changed because of it. Eventually, I realized that my fear of rejection was largely gone. As I reflect on this now, I can see how my newfound confidence, freedom, and willingness to take healthy risks and face rejection in various situations has come from my growing sense of God's love for me.

My wife, Sakiko, was raised in a well-to-do family and was popular at her school in Japan. Though she excelled in her academic, artistic, and athletic pursuits, she harbored deep pain because she did not feel loved. As I shared in my previous book,

Survival Guide for the Soul, Sakiko's parents had a daughter before she was born. When her mom became pregnant with Sakiko (in a time before ultrasound technology could determine the gender), her father declared, "This time, I want a boy."

When Sakiko was born, her disappointed dad said, "Let's just leave her at the hospital." Like many men of his generation, her dad was busy with his career and hardly ever home, so she felt neglected by him.

Just after college, Sakiko came to know Christ.

One day, out of the blue, she heard a voice tell her spirit, "You are Isaac."

It felt strange because Isaac is a boy's name. Later, as she was reading Genesis, she discovered that Isaac was born to Abraham and Sarah in their old age, after they had struggled with infertility for decades. Having longed to have a child for so many years, Sakiko knew that Isaac was a much-wanted and loved child. As Sakiko read this story, she felt God saying to her, "You are my longed-for and loved child."

This knowledge of being loved by God began to change her life.

When her dad died unexpectedly a couple of years ago, she felt deep sadness and anger about not feeling loved by him. Her dad never abused her and had many good qualities—including being a good provider. But she didn't feel *loved* by him.

Sakiko expressed this honestly to God, saying, "I wasn't loved by my dad and that makes me sad. You comfort me in many ways, but I still feel sad."

Then she heard God say, "But I love you."

And her heart was filled with a sense of contentment.

Knowing she is loved by God has fostered a sense of security and peace within her that she did not have previously.

Regardless of your background, you also can experience the love of God in a personal and profound way. My prayer in writing this book is that you would begin to have a deepening sense of God's love for you.

When you truly know that you are loved by God, you will not only become more willing to take risks and face possible rejection and failure, but you'll also be more resilient because you will feel buffered and protected by the One who upholds the whole universe. And in the presence of this vast, abundant, unconditional love, shame cannot survive.

When you are secure in God's love, you will also discover that you are becoming more of your true self—who you were before the world told you who you had to be. As you uncover your false self and let your masks fall away, the light of God will illuminate the brilliant diamond of your true self!

Love That Cannot Be Forfeited

You don't have to be a good student or a devoted or dutiful daughter or son to win God's love. No matter what you've done—or not done—you can never forfeit God's love for you.

Stefan grew up in a small town in Manitoba in the Canadian prairies.

He was raised in what he describes as an ideal home, where he was deeply loved by both his father and mother, who were committed followers of Jesus. When Stefan was ten years old, his mother was diagnosed with a serious, life-threatening illness and expected to die.

As a young boy, Stefan raged at God for this seeming unfairness and decided he would do everything he could to hurt God.

First, he began stealing and vandalizing the neighborhood.

Then in his adolescence, he started taking drugs. A few years later, he became a drug dealer. He treated others in demeaning and abusive ways and engaged in risky, promiscuous sex. When he was eighteen, his girlfriend of three months, Louise, became pregnant. They didn't want the baby and tried to abort it by having Louise take massive amounts of drugs, but she carried her baby to term.

After she went into labor at home, Stefan drove to the front entrance of the hospital, planning to drop Louise off and leave her in the hospital alone. But a nurse in his small town, where most people know each other, sensed his plans to flee. She approached the driver's side of his car and said, "Either dad comes in or I call your parents."

Reluctantly, he entered the delivery room of the hospital.

Stefan and Louise had already made plans for the baby to be adopted, so when the baby was about to be born, Stefan said he had no desire to see him. But the instant the baby was born, Stefan said, "I looked at him and it's like I'm looking at a miniature of me. I'm flooded with overwhelming emotions as I think about my early childhood innocence, but I can't make sense of what's going on." Then a clear thought came to his mind: "Stefan, the feeling you're experiencing is love and it pales in comparison to the love that I have for you." Knowing immediately that he was hearing God, he began weeping.

At first, Stefan struggled to accept God's love for him

because of his thievery, drug use and dealing, abuse of others, and attempt to kill his unborn child. But in time, he began to receive God's unconditional love, which changed his life and Louise's life, as well as the life of his son, Austin. At the time of this writing Austin is eighteen years old, with a heart to serve God and love others.

Stefan's mystical encounter with God in the hospital radically changed the direction of his life. After his son was born, he eventually quit dealing drugs, committed his life to God, married Louise, and became a pastor, helping others who are struggling with addiction and shame find freedom through God's love as he himself has.

While God may not speak to all of us in such a dramatic way, if we are receptive, he will reveal his love for us.

Becoming Receptive to God's Love

Do you ever find it difficult to access an awareness of God's love for you?

When I was in Taiwan, I spent time with an editor from the publishing company that published one of my previous books. He told me that God had never spoken to him through a voice or a vision. "For a long time," he confided, "I felt like such a mediocre, second-rate Christian." But then he read a book by Dallas Willard, a respected author on the spiritual life, who said that God can speak to us through our reason and thoughts. Looking back, he realized that God had in fact spoken to him through his thoughts and affirmed his love for him in various ways.

There are many ways God speaks to us through our reason

and thoughts, Scripture, and circumstances. Our deepest desires (with the exception of our addictions and infatuations) may also indicate God's will for us. God may at times even speak to us through the words and actions of people in our lives.

Sometimes, these experiences come out of the blue—as was the case for Sakiko and Stefan.

But we can also *invite* God to speak to us.

While teaching a class on being a disciple of Jesus at a Christian college, Deryck Livingstone asked, "Who has never really heard the Lord in a clear way?" A number of hands went up. "Would any of you like to ask God to speak to you?"

One young man named Ernest came forward, and Deryck prayed, "Lord, Ernest has come forward to hear your voice. Would you reveal yourself to him as he seeks you with all his heart?"

The class waited in silence, expectant and curious, but uncertain.

Ernest settled into the chair.

After a while, Deryck asked, "Ernest, has God laid anything on your heart?"

Ernest nodded and said softly, "He wants me to know how much he loves me."

Deryck asked, "Can you receive that?"

With some effort, Ernest said, "I've been trying so hard to do well in school, to make good choices, to please him." He paused, then said with wonder, "but he just wants me to know he really loves me, and all this other stuff doesn't matter that much."

When we slow down and make space to listen, God may speak to us, too[7] (see Jeremiah 29:13 and Matthew 7:7–8).

I have a friend here where I live in Vancouver whose wife

has been following Jesus since she was eleven. A few years ago, she realized that she had never asked God if he specifically loved her. So every day, she started asking, "Do you love me, Jesus?" It wasn't demanding or accusatory, and it didn't have a time limit. She just wanted to hear from him about herself.

After a month of persisting in this prayer, she read a familiar passage describing Jesus's suffering on the cross. "I know this," she thought. "I don't want to read it again." As she continued reading the passage, she felt a strong impression of words that were not her own, "I died so that I could be with you forever." These ten words now hang at the entrance to her home.

Spiritual Practices

Spiritual disciplines can help us open our eyes to the reality of God's love, which is all around us—like the air we breathe—but which we often don't perceive. Psychologists describe this ability to receive affirmation as a "receptive affect." Through meditative prayer exercises, we invite God to expand the receptive affect of our heart so we have a greater capacity to receive his affirmation and love.

Centering prayer, which I describe more fully in *Survival Guide for the Soul*,[8] can provide space for the Holy Spirit to help us excavate and release the things that may be blocking us from experiencing the love of God.

When we release our feelings of anxiety, fear, sadness, anger, and shame to God, we can become more receptive to the peace, rest, and love of God. Thus Thomas Keating, a deeply respected monk, describes centering prayer as "divine therapy."[9]

Through meditative prayer, we participate with God in the formation of our identity and the discovery of our beloved, true self. Thomas Merton says, "Our vocation is not simply to be, but to work together with God in the creation of our own life, our own identity, our own destiny."[10]

> *We tend to think that if we change, God will love us, but if we let God love us, we will change.*

While many of us *say* we believe God loves us, most of us *actually believe* that we're only in God's favor if we're good, keep the rules, and act responsibly. Or, we may *say* we believe God loves us, but *in practice*, we measure our worth by what we do, how much we achieve, and how others view us. But these are the measures of our false self rather than our true self.

When we truly *know* how deeply and unconditionally we are loved by God, it will not only change the way we see ourselves, but it will also change us. A Jesuit from India, Anthony de Mello, describes how he came to know that he was truly loved—and how it changed him:

> I was neurotic for years. I was anxious and depressed and selfish. Everyone kept telling me to change. I resented them and I agreed with them, and I wanted to change, but I simply couldn't, no matter how hard I tried.
>
> Then one day someone said to me, "Don't change. I love you just as you are." Those words were music to my ears. "Don't change. Don't change.
>
> Don't change . . . I love you as you are."
>
> I relaxed. I came alive. And suddenly I changed![11]

As a friend of mine reminds me, we tend to think that if we change, God will love us, but if we let God love us, we will change.

In the presence of perfect love, fear—including the fear of not measuring up and the fear of rejection—will be cast out, and the glory of the shimmering diamond of our true self will shine forth.

Prayer Exercise

My friend Curt Thompson, a psychiatrist and author, introduced me to the following meditative prayer practice, which helps me focus on the astonishing, far-reaching, enduring, and inclusive love of God, which is beyond measurement and transcends our understanding[12] (Ephesians 3:17–19 TPT).

Take a few deep breaths in and out of your nose.

Imagine you are in a beautiful place in nature—by the ocean or a lake, in a forest, a meadow, or the mountains.

Invite God's presence to be with you in this place.

Listen to the words God the Father says to Jesus at his baptism: "You are my Son, whom I love; with you I am well pleased" (Luke 3:22).

Now imagine hearing God speak these same words to you, calling you by name and saying, "_____, you are my *daughter/son*, whom I love; with you I am well pleased." Repeat this affirmation two more times.

These words are not only for Jesus but also for each of us.[13] If you have trouble believing you are as loved as the Father loves Jesus, remember Jesus tells all his disciples, "As the Father has loved me, so have I loved you" (John 15:9). The Hebrew prophet Zephaniah declares God "will take great delight in you; and in his love he will . . . rejoice over you with singing" (Zephaniah 3:17).

I invite you to practice this meditation for the next six weeks. As you do, it will not only affect you spiritually but physically as well. It will begin to change the neural networks in your brain, making you physiologically more receptive to the felt experience of God's love for you.

At first, you might experience this deeper awareness of being known and cared for by your Father in heaven only during the meditative prayer time itself. But over time, you may find that your capacity to receive God's love is expanding, and you will begin to receive positive images, words, feelings, and affirmations during the other moments of your life, including times of discomfort and discouragement. As you continue this practice, it will begin to transform the way you respond to your life experiences.

Reflection

After the Japanese-British novelist Kazuo Ishiguro won the Nobel Prize in literature, he said: "All I know is that I've wasted all these years looking for something. A sort of trophy I'd get if I really, really did enough to deserve it. But I don't want the trophy anymore. I want something else. Something warm and sheltering, something I can turn to regardless of what I do, regardless of who I become. Something that will just always be there like tomorrow's sky."[14]

"Something warm and sheltering" is a good description for the extravagant love of God, which he longs to pour over us until we are "filled to overflowing" and "flooding . . . with light."[15]

Study Guide Questions

1. If a child experiences secure attachment with a significant adult figure, what kind of capacities will they likely have? How can a child (or adult) who lives with insecure attachment patterns change from insecure to secure attachment?

2. How does being securely attached to God embolden us to take risks and face possible rejection?

3. Have you experienced a sense of God's love for you? If so, how?

4. Is there a practice that might help you expand your "receptive affect" for God's love (your capacity to receive God's love)?

Chapter 4

SEEING GOD'S FACE IN OTHERS

To love another person is to see the face of God.
—JEAN VALJEAN, *LES MISÉRABLES*

When one of my uncles was in his fifties, he took early retirement from his executive position at a bank in Vancouver. Though he had never gone to art school, he decided to pursue an avocation as a visual artist. Before his first public art exhibit at a gallery in Vancouver, he felt both excitement and anxiety. If no one bought a single painting and the reviews by the art critics were all bad, it would be virtually impossible for him to regard himself as a gifted artist. Sure, he could have rationalized that many of the greatest artists of history, including Van Gogh, were never recognized in their lifetimes. Even so, with no validation, my uncle could not have seen himself as a great artist.

We are not independent beings who can form our sense of self in isolation. We may say we don't care what other people think, but our sense of self is invariably shaped by how others respond to us—especially those who are closest to us. It is in relationships that our sense of self is formed. It is in relationships where we learn shame. And it is in relationship where our shame is undone.

In chapter 3, we reflected on how we can receive healing from shame through a personal experience of God's love. In this chapter, we're going to consider how we can know greater wholeness by experiencing divine love through others.

In the first century, followers of Jesus were publicly insulted because they believed Jesus, not Caesar, was the true emperor of the world. In some cases, because of their faith, they also lost their homes or had their animals and property confiscated (Hebrews 10:32–34).

In the midst of these shaming and discouraging circumstances, the writer of Hebrews penned the following words:

> Discover creative ways to encourage others and to motivate them toward acts of compassion, doing beautiful works as expressions of love. This is not the time to pull away and neglect meeting together, as some have formed the habit of doing. In fact, we should come together even more frequently, eager to encourage and urge each other onward as we anticipate that day dawning. (Hebrews 10:24–25 TPT)

Just as the followers of Christ in the first century had to encourage one another during their trials, we can help one another overcome our shame by building each other up through our presence, body language, and how we interact with and speak to one another.

Some have never experienced the power that words of life can bring to the soul, and others have only heard piercing words that bring death.[1]

I know a middle-aged man who is quite successful in his professional field, but he has a difficult time being vulnerable and presenting himself as less than perfect in the rest of his life. He remembers that when he was five years old, he walked into the kitchen of his family home while his mother was at the stove, cooking. "What are you making for dinner?" he asked. "Vegetables and chicken," his mother replied. The son asked, "Oh, can we have hot dogs, instead?" His mother grabbed him by the neck and yanked him outside, saying, "If you don't like my cooking, you're not going to eat." Slamming and locking the door, she added, "You're not having dinner tonight!"

The son cried out, "I am so sorry. I am so sorry. Please let me in! Please let me in! Please let me in!" Eventually, just before bedtime, the mother let her son back inside, but sent him to bed that night hungry, without dinner. This mother, though well-meaning and hard-working, was often harsh. To this day, this middle-aged man is overly eager to please others and will, at all costs, avoid provoking someone's anger.

We, too, may have had something said (or not said) to us that left us feeling a deficit.

Even if we don't consciously remember what was (or wasn't) said or done in our childhood or some other phase of our life, our experiences remain in our *implicit* memory and can continue to sway us.

How Implicit Memory Shapes Us

Dr. Clafard, a nineteenth-century neurologist, had a female patient whom he described as Madame X. The patient could chat about everyday events with her doctor, but if he left the room and returned a few minutes later, she would not recognize him nor remember their earlier conversation. He would have to reintroduce himself and begin again. Then one day Dr. Clafard hid a pin in his hand so that when he greeted Madame X and shook her hand, she received a sharp prick that caused her to cry out. At their next meeting, Dr. Clafard introduced himself as usual and extended his hand. Madame X pulled back and refused to shake it. When asked why, she said, "Sometimes doctors do things that hurt you."[2] This is implicit memory.

Though Madame X presented this as a fully conscious belief, its origins in the past were not accessible to her. What's more, the things we are unconscious of, our implicit memories, often have more power over us than our explicit memories.

Robert Bly, in *A Little Book on the Human Shadow*, says we carry around a backpack filled with shameful stories. He explains:

> [Our] parents wanted a nice girl or a nice boy. That's the first act of the drama. It doesn't mean our parents were wicked; they needed us for something. My mother, as a second-generation immigrant, needed my brother and me to help the family look more classy. We do the same thing to our children; it's a part of life on this planet. Our parents rejected who we were before we could talk, so the pain of the rejection is probably stored in some pre-verbal place.[3]

Bly says we carry a backpack full of shameful stories. Through loving interaction with a friend, family member, therapist, pastor, or spiritual director, our backpack filled with childhood shame can be re-narrated and our deficits can be transformed to become places of God-given grace.

Such healing can also occur in a small group.

The Power of Affirmation

Growing up, my friend Katie was loved by her parents, but because of issues stemming from their own childhoods, they couldn't be present in a way that made her feel attuned to or seen. In her adolescent years, whenever Katie pushed back on certain topics with her mother, her mother, who had vowed not to become violent like her own parents, always left the room.

In order for Katie not to feel cut off from her parents, she tried to become the version of herself that her mother wanted her to be. She found herself spiraling into a tailspin of shame that led to an eating disorder, which in her case was a symptom of her desire to disappear.

When she was eighteen, she went to see a therapist and sat with her knees up to her chest, hugging her legs, gazing at the floor. But thanks to this therapist's loving presence, which helped Katie feel seen and safe, she was eventually able to uncurl her body, make eye contact, connect, and find her voice.

Through the love and affirmation of her therapist and her friends, she came to understand more deeply the love of God and her own beauty and power, and over time she experienced healing and freedom.

Helping others feel seen and safe can have a powerful impact on their life so they can overcome their shame and reclaim their life. Psychologist John Bradshaw writes, "As infants we need to hear or *sense* someone saying to us, 'I'm so glad you're here. Welcome to the world!'" Bradshaw was aware, of course, that in many cases this does not happen, and so his therapeutic work included small groups of six to eight people (both males and females), who would give and receive words of affirmation to and from one another.

One by one, someone would sit in the center of the group and then direct the others as to how close to come. Some people wanted to be held, others preferred having group members place a hand gently upon their shoulders or back, and some preferred to have the group keep themselves at a little distance. Then Bradshaw would play some music, and each person in the circle would communicate a verbal affirmation to the person sitting in the center. Those who had been neglected often started sobbing when they heard the loving words they had never heard as a child. Those who had never received words of affirmation from their father were especially moved by hearing the male voices, and those who had never heard words of praise from their mother loved hearing the female voices.

Bradshaw observes that this kind of group exercise fosters powerful healing. Because shame involves being diminished or humiliated before others, we can overcome shame by honoring and validating people in front of others.[4]

I was recently in a similar small group exercise involving a circle where affirmations were given. I noticed that the affirmations became more creative as we went around the circle, because certain words of praise inspired a new encouragement from someone else. Becoming part of a small group at church can provide a context where we can receive, offer, and amplify God's affirmation and encouragement.

Growing Our Receptive Affect

These affirmation exercises also help people practice and develop what psychologists call the "receptive affect," which is the capacity to receive words of affirmation.

Many people have a difficult time receiving praise. They might lower their heads, saying, "No, no, no . . ." Or words of affirmation might bounce off their chest instead of sinking deep inside. When we receive affirmations from a small group or family member, a friend or pastor, spiritual director or counselor, we can practice this skill of stretching the receptive container inside us. These "drops of honey" can come to us in the form of uplifting words or a loving gaze or a reassuring touch.

Dr. Hillary McBride, a psychologist, told me that at some point in her therapy with someone, she'll say, "I'm going to tell you how I feel about you, and I want you to hold my gaze for just a little bit longer than you normally do."

She explains that, at first, the person may not be able to take in her words of encouragement or countenance of love and care. But over time, the person will be able to hold her gaze longer, and eventually some people can hold her gaze for several minutes. She adds, "You start with the five-pound dumbbell, move to ten pounds, and then on to twenty pounds, and work up to something heavier."

Through practice, we can expand our capacity to receive gifts of affirmation and blessing from others.

While some people find it hard to receive praise or a loving gaze from others, many find it even more difficult to experience affirmation from God because God is invisible. But if we learn to receive love from people, they can stand in for God and become "God's face" to us. When a person really sees us, we can say, "Oh, this is how God sees me." When a person deeply loves us, we can say, "This is how God loves me."

The Spanish mystic Teresa of Ávila wrote that as we become aware of the divine gaze of God, we become more like the God who gazes upon us. Just as we must be intentional about seeking to expand our "receptive affect," we also have to practice holding a loving gaze with God.

Receiving a loving, attentive gaze from someone also changes us on a physiological level, as it activates the limbic part of our brain and creates an "aha" moment.[5] Psychiatrist Curt Thompson points out that it takes less than three seconds for shame to form in our brain, but thirty to ninety seconds for an affirmation to form. When we attend to an affirming word or gaze, synapses fire and dopamine and serotonin are released

> *It takes less than three seconds for shame to form in our brain, but thirty to ninety seconds for an affirmation to form.*

in our brain, and over time, with repetition, we will be able to more easily access our neural pathways to joy. On an intuitive level, the apostle Paul understood this, and so in his letter on joy (written from prison), he urges us to dwell on whatever is true, noble, right, pure, lovely, admirable, excellent, or praiseworthy (Philippians 4:8).[6]

We can also deepen the effect of an affirming word or experience by writing the experience down. If I feel especially moved or uplifted by something, I will write it down or print it out and tape it into my journal.

The other night, I was going through an old journal and

came across a message that was sent by a friend about ten years ago:

> Ken,
>
> This doesn't happen to me a great deal, but I woke up at 4:30 this morning with a very clear sense I was to pray for you. I'm not sure why, but I did—and so I did.
>
> The image that came to me for you was one of God celebrating over you, in the sense not only that God loves you, but that he also LIKES you. He likes your walk, the way you talk, your sense of humor—even the things you feel are just odd or quirky—maybe even something you are wishing you could change about yourself, God likes.

I knew God loved me, but I hadn't thought much about whether God *liked* me, and this encouragement lifted me up and drew me closer to God. We may "know" something at an intellectual or intuitive level, but hearing the same truths from someone else can make a truth even more vivid to us.

Writing these encouraging or uplifting things down can reacquaint us with joy and help us travel further along the road of healing. I know someone who grew up receiving the false messages that he was dirty, stupid, and ugly. These inaccurate, demeaning messages filled him with anxiety and despair. As a young adult, a psychiatrist told him about the power of positive truth statements. She counseled, "Don't simply come up with them yourself, but go to your best friends and ask them to identify the qualities they see in you." So, he reached out to his best friends and then typed out their responses:

- "You have an amazing capacity to persevere through difficulties."
- "You are a role model and a leader to young men."
- "You are fun. You bring laughter."

He realized that these affirmations were harder to refute because others had expressed them. Now he reads them out loud, sometimes a few times a day. This "outside-in" healing over time has changed the way he sees and treats himself.

The experience of receiving affirmation from others is important because many of us fail to treat ourselves with the same level of respect, courtesy, and compassion with which we treat others.

A small experiment was conducted with a group of teenage girls and their sisters. The researcher asked the girls to write down any negative thoughts they had that affected their self-esteem. They wrote down things like, "you are scared," "you are worthless," "you are unimportant." Then he asked them to read what they had written about themselves to their sisters—as if it were directed at *them*. They all refused. "It's not very nice," one said. It was normal for her to say this to herself, but completely mean if she were saying it to someone else.[7] We may say terribly demeaning things to ourselves that we would never say to others!

Another gift that flows from a person treating us in an

> *When we take the risk of allowing ourselves to be seen—including the parts of us we feel are hideous and shameful—and the other person says, "I am not going anywhere," "I am not ashamed of you," or "Welcome to the human race," deep healing can occur.*

affirming and compassionate way is that we are more likely to treat ourselves with kindness and compassion.

My friend who got drunk and passed out on the sidewalk in Vancouver (see chapter 2, "Covered by Grace") received a profound experience of affirmation in the wake of his experience of failure and shame. When we take the risk of allowing ourselves to be seen—including the parts of us we feel are hideous and shameful—and the other person says, "I am not going anywhere," "I am not ashamed of you," or "Welcome to the human race," deep healing can occur.

The Practice of Confession

James Pennebaker, a professor at the University of Texas, studied what happens when trauma survivors, especially rape and incest survivors, kept their experiences secret. The research team found that the act of not discussing a traumatic event or confiding it to another person could be more damaging than the actual event. Conversely, when people shared their stories and experiences, their physical health improved, their doctor's visits decreased, and they showed significant declines in the activity of their stress hormones.[8]

My practice of confession with God and certain trusted people is one of the most powerful ongoing spiritual disciplines in my life. For most of us, the practice of confession is not easy. As a young adult, I joined a small group and knew we were going to be invited to share transparently. I was with people I could trust, but I was still afraid and blurted out, "I recently went skydiving for the first time. Jumping out of the airplane was difficult, but relatively easy compared to baring my soul." Sharing our innermost self is not easy, but it is the pathway to one of life's greatest gifts: deep friendship.

I am profoundly grateful for the safe space for confession that is created by my spiritual director, Dan. I am also thankful for my longtime friendship with Elizabeth, with whom I've been able to open my heart and feel received (and, at times, necessarily rebuked). I deeply value my weekly Zoom conversation with my friend Mark, where we mutually confess temptations, struggles, and sins, and then pray for each other. This may sound heavy, but in practice, it feels truly uplifting.

I first began to see the value of confession when I was single. During my student years, one summer break while traveling, I had a romantic fling. Neither of us could see ourselves with each other: she was in a relationship with someone else, and I was intending to initiate an exclusive dating relationship with someone back home. But that summer we found ourselves powerfully attracted to each other, and one night we crossed some lines. We were in a public space, so there was a natural restraint in place, but we ended up engaged in some prolonged kissing and making out.

You might think it's not a big deal, but I knew I had violated my conscience and was feeling guilt and shame. Not long after this, I confessed what I had done to a close friend and mentor. He was disappointed and teared up, but he also expressed his love for me, and I felt his profound care. Having confessed and been received with love, I felt an enormous burden lifting from my shoulders. When we can express our feelings and faults honestly with a safe person, something inside us lifts and straightens.

Dan Siegel, a researcher and professor of psychiatry at

UCLA, points out that when we confess something that is weighing on our heart in the presence of an empathetic person, the neurotransmitter GABA squirts into our brain, creating a calming effect.[9] Dr. Brené Brown's research also shows that one of the most effective strategies for shame resilience is to cultivate friendships with trusted people who can become sources of empathy.[10]

When we share a painful or shameful experience with someone we trust, we can begin to *reframe* our shame.

Sometime after my summer fling, I shared my experience with another wise friend. After listening pensively, he said, "I know you feel like you made a bad decision, but I also see that you demonstrated integrity in that situation by setting certain boundaries when you were given the opportunity to become even more physically intimate. A failure at this level may actually be beneficial for you. It may help you avoid something much more serious in the future."

Although I had still felt some residual guilt and shame over the experience, having the experience *reframed* for me caused the burden to lift even further and gave me a sense of deep gratitude.

Sharing our experiences of shame, pain, or grief can help us reframe our story. When we see it in a new light, we can even begin to view it as something redemptive and beautiful in the larger tapestry of our lives. This will certainly be true for those who believe in the God who redeems

> *"If you put shame in a petri dish, it needs three ingredients to grow exponentially: secrecy, silence, and judgment. If you put the same amount of shame in the petri dish and douse it with empathy, it can't survive."*[11]
>
> —Brené Brown

all things and makes *all things* in our life work together for our ultimate good—and his greater glory as we are transformed into the image of Christ.

Ideally, we will be able to disclose ourselves to someone we trust or to a professional with a credible reputation, but we can also find freedom by confessing to someone who is a relative stranger.

Auburn Sandstrom, a professor of writing at the University of Akron, shares her story of finding an unexpected confessor in a stranger:

> I was curled up in a fetal position on a filthy carpet in a cluttered apartment. I'm in horrible withdrawal from a drug addiction. I have a little piece of paper. It's dilapidated because I've been folding it and unfolding it. But I could still make out the phone number on it.
>
> I am in a state of bald terror. My husband is out, and trying to get a hold of some of the drugs that we needed. But right behind me, sleeping in the bedroom, is my baby boy. I wasn't going to get a Mother of the Year award. In fact, at the age of 29, I was failing at a lot of things. So, I decided to get clean. I was soon going to lose the most precious thing I'd ever had in my life—that baby boy.
>
> I was so desperate at that moment that I wanted to make use of that phone number—it was something my mother had sent me. She said, "This is a Christian counselor, maybe sometime you could call this person."
>
> It was 2 in the morning, but I punched in the numbers. I heard a man say, "Hello." And I said, "Hi, I got this number from my mother. Uh, do you think you could

maybe talk to me?" He said, "Yes, yes, of course. What's going on?"

I told him I was scared, and that my marriage had gotten pretty bad. Before long, I started telling him other truths, like I might have a drug problem. And this man just sat with me and listened and had such a kindness and a gentleness. "Tell me more . . . Oh, that must hurt very much." And he stayed up with me the whole night, just being there until the sun rose. By then I was feeling calm. The raw panic had passed. I was feeling OK.

I was very grateful to him, and so I said, "I really appreciate you and what you've done for me tonight. How long have you been a Christian counselor?" There's a long pause. He said, "Auburn, please don't hang up. I'm so afraid to tell you this . . . He pauses again. "You got the wrong number. I'm not a therapist, but I've really enjoyed talking with you."

I didn't hang up on him. I never got his name. I never spoke to him again. But the next day I felt like I was shining. I discovered that there was this completely random love in the universe. That it could be unconditional. And that some of it was for me. And it also became possible as a teetotaling, single parent to raise up that precious baby boy into a magnificent young scholar and athlete, who graduated from Princeton with honors. In the deepest, blackest night of despair, if you can get just one pinhole of light . . . all of grace rushes in.[12]

When Auburn was able to share the truth about her life—her fear, addiction, and shame—with another person, even though he wasn't a trained counselor, she found a pinhole of light and a flood of grace. When she told the truth and entrusted her story to another person, she discovered an "unconditional" love—a love that did not run away from her shame, but vanquished it, allowing her true self to shine forth.

When a person knows our shame and then loves us and receives us, the shame cannot survive. In the sacred space of unconditional love, we become our true self, and the shimmering diamond of who we really are gleams brighter.

Prayer Exercise

———◇———

Take several deep breaths, breathing in and out of your nose.

When you feel still and peaceful, return to the prayer exercise from the end of chapter 3. Continue to meditate on the words God the Father says to Jesus at his baptism, imagining that God is speaking these words to you: (insert your name) "_____, you are my *daughter/son*, whom I love. I am so pleased with you. I delight that you are on the earth" (Luke 3:22).

After listening to these words of love, practice holding a loving gaze with God by listening for any other affirmations God might want to speak into your heart. Breathe deeply, inhaling *you are my daughter/son*, and exhaling, *whom I love*. After listening, take a moment to write down any affirmations you may want to remember.

Now invite God to expand your capacity to receive affirmations from others by bringing to your mind the names and faces of people who have blessed you and loved you into being. After breathing and listening quietly, give thanks for each of these people. Then write down any words of affirmation you may have received from them.

Reflection

As we seek to uncover the shimmering diamond of our true self, we may need to reacquaint ourselves with our pathways of joy. Regardless of our current circumstances, we can intentionally seek to "fix our thoughts on what is true, and honorable, and right, and pure, and lovely, and admirable. [And] think about things that are excellent and worthy of praise" (Philippians 4:8 NLT).

Study Guide Questions

1. How has your sense of self been shaped by others?
2. In what ways have explicit and implicit childhood memories formed you?
3. How can the presence, body language, and words of others help us experience healing from shame?
4. What practice or posture might help you expand your capacity to receive the affirmation of others?
5. How might confession with a trusted, empathetic person bring healing? How can you make confession a regular practice in your life?
6. How can you seek to reflect God's face to others?

Chapter 5

MASTERPIECE IN
THE MAKING

*We believe, if I behave correctly, I will one day get
God to love me or even notice me. We tend toward this
behavioral model. But the biblical tradition actually
teaches that first we must see God clearly, often by
experiencing God's mercy for our bad behavior—and
then our right behavior will follow. We first must
encounter and experience God's original blessing,
choosing, and loving of us. If you start with original
sin or shame, normally the pit is so deep you never
get out of it.*

—RICHARD ROHR[1]

A number of years ago, my wife and I were visiting Rome.
As we looked across this ancient city one evening, we saw
the Roman Colosseum in the distance, and the words "magnificent ruin" came to my mind.[2] Because we have been created
in the image of God, we are "magnificent," but we have also
experienced the "ruin" of sin and shame.

If you were raised in the church, you were likely taught that all human beings are sinners. Perhaps you've heard of the doctrine of original sin, which teaches that ever since Adam and Eve turned away from God in the garden of Eden, we humans have been prone to wander from God.

Though we are prone to sin and stray from God, it is important to remember that before original sin, we were clothed with *original glory.* God longs for humankind to experience the full restoration of our original glory, which we enjoyed at the beginning of creation.

In Scripture, Paul says that we are being made into God's masterpiece, as we are created anew in Christ Jesus (Ephesians 2:10 NLT). What does it mean to become God's masterpiece?

Part of this surely means growing in holiness.

In Scripture, the apostle Peter writes, "But just as he who called you is holy, so be holy in all you do; for it is written: 'Be holy, because I am holy'" (1 Peter 1:15–16). When we are finally restored to our original glory, we will be "holy in all [we] do" (1 Peter 1:15).

If you were raised in a religious community, you probably associate holiness with rules and regulations, behavior, and morality. While how we live certainly matters, the *strong emphasis* on behavior and morality in Christianity does not come so much from Jesus or the biblical narrative, but largely from the eighteenth-century German philosopher, Immanuel Kant.[3] Kant's influential concept of the categorical imperative emphasized our moral obligation to obey divine commands not because of an immediate good that would result or some future reward or punishment, but simply because they were commands from God.

Respected theologian N. T. Wright argues that our primary emphasis as Christians should be on restoring the image of God within us rather than obeying rules and regulations. We don't need to *emphasize* obeying rules, because as the Spirit fills us, we will naturally grow in holiness and wholeness.[4] As we are filled with the life and love of God, the divine image is restored within us, and we will grow more like God: more whole, more holy, more beautiful. Just as those who eat well become physically healthier and can absorb nutritious food more readily, when we grow more whole, our receptive capacity for God expands, and divine holiness and beauty are restored within us. We find ourselves on a virtuous, transformative cycle in which we emerge out of the shadows of sin and shame into our true self.

Do you have a vision of being set apart for God—being made whole, holy, and beautiful—so you can become your truest self, God's masterpiece? We can cultivate a vision for becoming God's masterpiece by knowing our true identity and that our *original* state was full of God's glory and blessing rather than sin.

Envisioning Our Future Self

Several years ago, our church staff researched our individual family trees as part of a team building exercise. While tracing my father's lineage back to the 1800s, I discovered that my ancestors were Japanese samurai. Samurai are typically portrayed as warriors deftly wielding swords in battle. But historically, when they were not required to defend their community, they worked as farmers, philosophers, poets, teachers, and artists.

My forebears were teachers of Confucian literature and ethics to the lords of the Samurai clan.

In my vocation as a pastor and spiritual teacher, I am energized by knowing that I am doing something in continuity with my ancestors, who are expressing themselves through me as I bear their genetic code and something of their spirit. When our identity is rooted in the knowledge that we are the offspring of creatures who were made by God in dazzling glory and created with an original core of goodness and beauty, we can live inspired to become the masterpieces God intended.

When we catch a vision for who we might become in the future, we can begin to live as that person now.

But this future version of ourselves, far on the horizon, can look like a stranger to us. Hal Ersner-Hershfield, a psychologist at New York University, wondered if young adults were not saving money for the future because they felt like they were putting it away for a stranger. So he conducted an experiment, giving some college students a real mirror and others virtual reality goggles where, with the help of special effects like those used in movies, they could see a future version of themselves at age 68 or 70. Those who saw the older version of themselves in the virtual "mirror" were willing to put more than twice as much money into their retirement accounts as the students who spent time looking at their younger selves in a real mirror. What's more, those who glimpsed their future selves were more likely to complete their studies on time, whereas those who didn't were more likely to blow off their studies. Those who saw their future selves were also more likely to act ethically in business scenarios.[5]

When we can imagine ourselves in both our temporal future

and our eternal future, we can be inspired toward holiness in our day-to-day lives. In his classic sermon "The Weight of Glory," C. S. Lewis observes, "There are no *ordinary* people." He continues, "Remember that the dullest, most uninteresting person you can talk to may one day be a creature which, if you saw it now, you would be strongly tempted to worship, or else a horror and a corruption such as you now meet, if at all, only in a nightmare. All day long we are, in some degree, helping each other to one or the other of these destinations."[6] As the theologian N. T. Wright observes, when we think of an older, physically diminished person, we might say, "They are just a shadow of their former self," but when someone belongs to Christ, we should say, "They are just a shadow of their *future* self."[7]

If you can envision your future, glorious self, you can move toward becoming that person right now, bearing the beautiful image of God in your daily life.

Consenting to Holiness

As we grow into the glorious masterpieces of God's imagining, we aren't embarking on a pull-ourselves-up-by-our-bootstraps self-improvement project.

Rather, we are opening ourselves to be shaped by God's creative, loving hands, inviting him to use whatever tools are necessary to slough away our dross. For it is only after we pass through purifying fire, after God chisels, sands, and burnishes us, that we will begin to shimmer with an inner radiance that will cast warmth and light upon everyone around us.

Though this creative process is something that God does as

an artist—as Jesus said, "apart from [him] [we] can do nothing" (John 15:5)—we also play a role (Philippians 2:13).

Our role is to consent to the cleansing work of the Holy Spirit.

When I was a teenager, I kept a pornographic magazine hidden behind one of the logs stacked in our garage. When I first met Christ, I knew nothing about the Bible, and I hadn't yet heard about the Holy Spirit. But as soon as the Spirit made a home within me, my first instinct was to grab the pornographic magazine I'd hidden behind the log, toss it into the fireplace of our living room, and burn it. I had an inward sense, born of the Spirit, that pornography would compromise my new relationship with God.

In due course, I also felt an inner urge to make things right with certain kids whom I had bullied in our neighborhood and at my high school. As humbling as it was, I felt that I needed to go to them and ask them to forgive me for the way I had treated them. Though imperfectly, I was saying yes to the work of the Holy Spirit in me.

Decades later, with God's help, I still seek to respond to the Holy Spirit within me, whether by making a choice not to objectify an attractive woman, or to initiate repair and reconciliation in a fractured relationship, or to respond to a conviction of sin in some other area of my life. We do not need to fear these inner urgings because the Holy Spirit never condemns us, but gently convicts us.[8] Condemnation drives us from God, but conviction draws us toward God.

For many of us, the temptation to sin might not come most often in obvious areas, such as sexual lust or the desire to dominate or bully someone, but in more subtle inclinations. For example, like many people, I am inclined to place too much security in my bank balance and what I have accumulated rather than trusting in God's provision. By nature, I also have a tendency to base my self-worth on how I perform at work and in other spheres of life. Or I can become overly attached to someone and then start trying a little too hard to impress them. In certain situations, I also feel an anxious desire to influence or control the outcome. Although I play a role in my transformation, I am ultimately powerless to change these tendencies in myself.

> *Experiencing real change is not just a matter of willpower or intellectual insight—we need God to do a cleansing and transformative work within us.*

On our own, we cannot experience freedom from our attachments and addictions to security, affection, esteem, power, and control. Our primal desires for these things are wired into our central nervous system, deeply rooted in our bodies. As Thomas Keating says, "our issues are in our tissues."[9] Experiencing real change is not just a matter of willpower or intellectual insight—we need God to do a cleansing and transformative work within us.

This is why I pray this simple welcoming prayer I have adapted from Mary Mrozowski. I pray this prayer each morning as part of a time of meditation. I may also pray it at various points in the day as I feel unhealthy frustration and desire for security, validation, or control:

> *I consent to the work of the Holy Spirit.*
> *I let go of my desire for security and pleasure.*

I let go of my desire for affection and esteem.
I let go of my desire for power and control.[*]

I invite you to consider regularly praying this welcoming prayer if you want to become a person who does not make your money, your work, pleasure, food, what others think of you, or your influence and power your functional god. Becoming God's masterpiece is primarily God's work in us, and so our role is to *consent* to the work of the Holy Spirit. Sometimes we respond and agree to the Holy Spirit's work of removing sin from our lives; at other times we allow the Spirit to declutter us.

When Sakiko and I clean our home, we toss out all our garbage (used Kleenex, socks with too many holes, blueberries turning white with mold, and so on). Each summer, we do a deeper cleaning, going through our closets and identifying clothes that we haven't worn for a year to give them to the Salvation Army Thrift Store. We also browse our bookshelves, culling any we won't read again, and donate them to a nearby library or used bookstore. Recently, while we were cleaning out our garage, Sakiko found some wedding gifts in storage containers that we hadn't used in nearly two decades—so we gave them to the Salvation Army. When we throw away our garbage and give away things we're not using anymore, we get rid of the clutter in our house, and this opens more space for the things we need and value.

---

[*] Pamela Begeman, Mary Dwyer, Cherry Haisten, Gail Fitzpatrick-Hopler, and Therese Saulnier, *The Welcoming Prayer: Consent on the Go, a 40-Day Praxis* (West Milford, NJ: Contemplative Outreach, 2018). Prayer used with permission. If you are interested in learning more about the booklet, please go to the website of Contemplative Outreach at www.contemplativeoutreach.org/product/the-welcoming-prayer-consent-on-the-go-a-40-day-praxis/.

If we want to become the masterpieces God created us to be, we will invite the Holy Spirit to help us declutter our lives by removing things that might not be bad in and of themselves but occupy space or time that could be put to better use.

For example, Sakiko and I had a Netflix account we weren't using very often. Occasionally I felt compelled to watch something to justify the subscription price. Eventually, we canceled our subscription so we could direct that money toward something we valued more.

According to author Jay Shetty, a typical person today will spend more than eleven years of his or her lifetime on screens, looking at TV and social media.[10] Many of us would do well to limit our screen time intentionally so we can create space in our lives for more important priorities.

By nature, I enjoy activity and thrive with a certain level of pressure, but I also know that if I say yes to too many opportunities and take on too many responsibilities, my relationship with God and the most important people in my life will suffer. In the classic *Testament of Devotion*, Thomas Kelly counsels that unless there is a Divine yes from our Center, say no so you don't get too busy.[11]

> *Unless there is a Divine yes from our Center, say no so you don't get too busy.*

If we want to experience the deep transformation of the master artist, we need to make space in our minds and hearts to attend to God's loving presence. This will include opening ourselves to the purifying work of the Holy Spirit in relation to possible sin in our lives and inviting Jesus to cleanse our bodies and spirits of any garbage or clutter that might distract us from his presence.

Body Scan

For me, the most transformative way I do this, as I described in a previous chapter, is by setting aside some time for prayerful meditation each morning. Typically, I commit about twenty minutes for silent meditative prayer. This always includes breathing in deeply through my nose and exhaling slowly through my nose. The biblical Hebrew word for breath and spirit are one and the same. As I breathe in, I am conscious that I am breathing in the very breath or Spirit of God. As I breathe in, I may pray, "Fill me with your Spirit, Lord."

While engaging in this meditative prayer, I often invite God literally to have every part of my body. Starting with my feet, I tighten my muscles, then relax and offer my feet to God. Moving up through each part of my body, I tighten and then relax the muscles in my ankles, shins, calves, thighs, groin, hips, abdomen, chest, shoulders, upper arms, forearms, and hands, offering each part to God. Finally, I scan my neck, mouth, nose, eyes, ears, and head, offering each to God.

This body-scan prayer is a way for me to tangibly offer my body as a living sacrifice, set apart for God (Romans 12:1–2).

Transformed by Love

Thomas Merton once asked, "How does an apple get ripe?"

The answer? By simply sitting in the sun.[12]

The great saints described this practice of "sitting in the sun" as "resting" in the "gaze of God."

When we catch a glimpse of someone looking at us in love,

it changes us on a physiological level. When we experience the "gaze of God," we are transformed on both a neurobiological and a spiritual level.

We can practice resting in the gaze of God through prayerful meditation, gratitude practices, keeping a Sabbath rhythm, spending time in nature, or hanging out with friends. As we attune to God's gaze upon us, we will feel more deeply beloved, which will wash away our shame and help us reflect the loving, compassionate gaze of God to others.

In Scripture, Paul writes that when we, with unveiled faces, contemplate the Lord's glory, we are "being transformed into his image with ever-increasing glory" (2 Corinthians 3:18). In our own time, this truth has been corroborated by neurobiologists, who have found that we become like the objects of our attention. As Daniel Siegel, a researcher and professor of psychiatry at UCLA, says, "Where attention goes, neural firing flows, and neural connection grows."[13]

Some people may feel that it is dangerous to meditate on a God who receives you without condition and loves you so deeply that you actually can't do *anything* to make him love you more or less. And if you fail, a God who won't leave. This message about God seems dangerous because it might encourage some people to take advantage of God and live irresponsibly.

But Scripture tells us that "God's *kindness* is intended to lead you to repentance" (Romans 2:4, emphasis mine).

If a young boy is naturally rebellious but grows to understand how deeply he is loved by his parents and believes they have his best interests at heart, he is more likely to trust, honor, and obey his parents than a child who constantly feels threatened by his parents or unsure of their love.

Canadian psychologist David Benner describes a patient named "Amanda," who was fifteen years old when she entered therapy with him after her third suicide attempt in three months. When Benner met Amanda, she was dressed head to toe in black and had large, black circles painted around her eyes. Her face and ears were riddled with studs and rings, and she was wearing a dog collar, which was attached to a waist belt with a conspicuous industrial-grade chain.

When Benner introduced himself, Amanda did not acknowledge his presence, but she got up and followed him into his office, along with the woman sitting beside her. In the office, the woman introduced herself as Amanda's mother. Turning to Amanda, Benner asked if she was willing to have her mother accompany her for this consultation. Amanda said that her mother was her best friend and had come because she had invited her.

Young people like Amanda are typically not best friends with their mothers, and yet the affection between them was clear. Sensing that the mother disapproved of her daughter's lifestyle, Benner asked Amanda what had enabled her to remain so close to her mother despite their differences. Amanda replied, "For as long as I can remember, every night of my life, I ended the day by going to bed with my mother and snuggling."

Amanda's remarkable relationship with her mother enabled her to leave behind what she describes now as her "black period" and to find her way through adolescence in a relatively healthy manner. Amanda knew that she was deeply loved exactly as she was. Her mother disapproved of her drug use, promiscuous sex, foul language, Satanic practices, and most other aspects of her lifestyle. But with wisdom rarely seen in parents, this mother recognized what her daughter needed most were not lectures, but love. Fortunately, she had been giving Amanda large doses of love throughout Amanda's life, and she did not allow her disapproval of her daughter's behavior to disrupt this pattern.

Amanda's mother offered a truly transforming love, because even though her daughter might resist it, the fact that she continued to receive it had a profound psychological and spiritual impact on her.[14]

Encountering God's Love: Discovering Our Original Glory

God doesn't love us because we are good but because *God is good.*

When we really believe God is good and God loves us and has our best interests at heart, we will change. We will be more likely to surrender ourselves to God and seek to honor him and his good design for us.

> *God doesn't love us because we are good but because God is good.*

At the beginning of this chapter, I quoted Richard Rohr, a Franciscan priest, who says that before we emphasize "behave correctly," we must *first* "see God clearly." Most of us will only be able to see God clearly after we experience God's mercy for our bad behavior—and then our right behavior will follow. Rohr's words are worth repeating here: "We first must encounter and experience God's original blessing, choosing, and loving of us. If you start with original sin or shame, normally the pit is so deep you never get out of it."

When I realize that God loves me even in my worst moments—when I am not growing, not obeying—I am inspired to live with more faithfulness. God's kindness humbles me, fills me with gratitude, and leads me to repentance.

In a letter to the church in Rome, Paul asks, "What should be our proper response to God's marvelous mercies?" Then he answers his own question, instructing the Christians to "surrender yourselves to God to be his sacred, living sacrifices. And live in holiness, experiencing all that delights his heart. For this becomes your genuine expression of worship" (Romans 12:1–2 TPT).

We can overcome our sense of shame and our feeling of not being enough by inviting the Spirit to clear sin from our lives so we can be set apart for God and become holy vessels filled with the light of his glory.

Then the grand artist can shape us into the beautiful, complete masterpieces God imagined long before we were born.

When Sakiko and I were visiting Rome, we spent time in the Sistine Chapel, where Michelangelo completed his masterpiece in 1512. In those days, the only source of light came from candles, and year after year, the soot from all those candles rose to the ceiling. After more than four hundred years of soot, grime, and dust collecting on the ceiling, the original paintings had become obscured. So, it was widely believed that Michelangelo's use of color was mediocre—too dull and dark. But then, between 1984 and 1989, a team of restorative artists worked to restore the paintings on the ceiling to their original beauty, revealing an array of bright spring colors: cherry blossom pink, apple green, sunny yellow, and sky blue against a background of luminescent gray.

Many of us are covered with the soot, grime, and dust of our lives, and God is longing to restore us to our original glory. In time, as we are unveiled by his restoring work, we will be transformed into the beautiful masterpiece he created us to be—one of ever-increasing glory (2 Corinthians 3:18).

Prayer Exercise

———◇———

Take several deep breaths, breathing in and out of your nose.

When you feel still and peaceful, return once more to the prayer exercise from the end of chapter 3. Continue to meditate on the words God the Father says to Jesus at his baptism, imagining God is speaking these words to you: "_____, you are my *daughter/son*, whom I love; with you I am well pleased." After listening to these words of love, invite God, the artist of your soul, to restore you to your original glory, the beautiful, beloved masterpiece you were created to be. Breathe deeply, inhaling, *you are my daughter/son*, and exhaling, *whom I love*.

Now invite God's Spirit to reveal any "clutter" in your life that needs to be removed. Then ask if there are any practices the artist of your soul is stirring you to embrace so you can rest more fully in the gaze of God's love.

Reflection

When Jesus died on the cross, he himself bore your sins in his body, breaking the power of sin and death so that you might live to righteousness; for by his wounds *you have been healed* (1 Peter 2:24).

Study Guide Questions

1. How can you root your identity in your *original glory*? How might this inspire you to holiness more than emphasizing rules and regulations?
2. How can you cultivate a future vision of yourself? How might this make you more beautiful?
3. How can you *consent* to holiness in your daily life?
4. Where do you see God shaping you and inviting you to embrace the holy?
5. How can you focus on seeing God's mercy more clearly in your daily life? Do you sense a posture or practice you are being called to embrace so you can become a masterpiece?

Chapter 6

OVERCOMING ENVY

Envy is when you resent God's goodness in other people's
lives and ignore God's goodness in your own life.
—CRAIG GROESCHEL

A number of years ago, I was speaking at a Christian fellowship at Harvard. As one of the student leaders drove me to the campus, I inquired, "What advice can you give me about speaking to the students?" He replied, "Harvard students struggle with feeling significant."

"Are you kidding?" I asked. "If *I* had been accepted to Harvard, I think all my self-esteem issues would be over."

"It's not that way at all," he explained. "There are so many talented people here, it's hard to stand out."

If you were a bona fide supermodel, you would probably feel good about your body, right? But supermodel Cameron Russell said she's never met a model who didn't feel insecure about their body. How can this be? Because supermodels compare themselves with other models, whose bodies they regard as superior to their own.[1]

If you were making $500,000 a year, do you think you would feel content with your salary? You would be in the top

1 percent of all people in North America—and far ahead of most people in the world. But if you were earning $500,000 a year as a professional baseball player for the Los Angeles Angels, you might feel insecure when you learned that one of your teammates, Mike Trout, had recently signed a contract for nearly half a billion dollars to stay with the team for another twelve years.[2]

Comparison, Envy, and Shame

When we compare ourselves to people who have accomplished more than we have, we feel insignificant. But most of us don't compare ourselves to a king or queen—they may inhabit the same planet, but they live in a completely different world. Instead, we tend to measure ourselves against those who are part of our family, neighborhood, school, workplace, or professional field—people we can easily identify with in some way.

Comparison gives birth to the twins of envy and shame. Envy is the resentful feeling that someone else either is or has it better than me; shame is the feeling that naturally follows envy when we think "I'm not enough" and "What's wrong with me?"

A friend makes more money than we do, and we envy them.

A classmate gets better grades than we do, and we feel dumb in comparison.

We are jealous of a teammate who is in better shape than we are.

We are aging and envy everyone who looks healthier or younger than we look.

We are single and envy a friend who has a partner.

We feel stuck in a bad marriage and envy a coworker who is single and free—or a friend who has a *better* spouse.

We are struggling with infertility and feel less than our friends who have children.

We have a son who is struggling in school, and we feel resentful when we hear our sister talk about how well her daughter is doing.

We feel our lives are bogged down by our children and begin to begrudge people who don't have children because they seem to have so much freedom.

We rent an apartment and envy our sister, who owns a house. Or we own a small house and envy our brother, who has a much bigger house in a much better neighborhood. Or we own a big house, but we envy a cousin who owns a house *and* several vacation homes.

All these comparisons spawn feelings of envy toward others and shame about ourselves, making us feel that we don't quite measure up and are inadequate in some way.

Envy is one of the seven deadly sins and is considered to be the most widely experienced of the seven—but it is also the sin that people are least likely to confess. It's embarrassing to confess that we envy someone. Yet envy has become even more pervasive in our age of social media, when it is so easy to compare our lives to someone else's highlight reel and then feel like we don't show up in a favorable light. With so much media saturation, it's easier than ever before to make unfavorable comparisons.

As historian Yuval Noah Harari points out, if you were an eighteen-year-old youth in a small village 5,000 years ago, you would probably think you were good-looking because there were only fifty other males in your village, and most of them were either old, scarred, and wrinkled, or they were still little kids.

But if you are a teenager today, you are more likely to feel inadequate. And if you think the other guys at your school are an ugly lot, you don't measure yourself against them. You measure yourself against the movie stars, professional athletes, and supermodels you see all day on television, social media, and giant billboards.[3]

In the Bible, we can see this dynamic in the relationship between Saul and David. As a young shepherd in Israel, David was not widely known—some even thought of him as a nobody. But after he hurled a stone from his sling and slew the giant Goliath—the archenemy and menace of his people—he became a *somebody*. So King Saul sends David to lead military campaigns, and David becomes a stunning success.

So stunning that when he and his men return home from battle, the women of Israel come out of their houses, dancing, shaking tambourines, and singing, "Saul has slain his thousands, and David his tens of thousands" (1 Samuel 18:7). Hearing this song, Saul experiences the torment of envy and the accompanying emotion of shame. As he considers his life alongside David's, he feels as if he's not enough. Sensing that he has been surpassed by David, Saul envies him so intensely that he later hurls a spear at him—twice—thinking, "I'll pin David to the wall" (v. 11).

As this story reminds us—along with the biblical stories of archetypal brothers such as Cain and Abel, or Jacob and Esau—envy has been part of the human condition since the fall.

Researcher Frans de Waal wondered if other mammals experience envy, so he trained capuchin monkeys to use stones as a sort of currency, trading a stone for a slice of cucumber. The monkeys were perfectly content with this arrangement as long as they were all getting the same thing—a slice of cucumber in exchange for a stone. Then de Waal changed the social dynamic and gave one monkey a sweet grape instead of the cucumber slice. The monkey in the cage beside him lost his temper and threw his cucumber slice in the face of the trainer and then shook his cage in rage.[4]

You may ask how this is relevant. Certainly, we are different from monkeys and other higher primates! In many ways we are, but when it comes to our propensity to compare and feel envy, perhaps not so much.

Or consider another study in which researchers examined data from millions of plane flights to determine possible indicators for incidences of "air rage"—when passengers become unruly, disruptive, or violent in some way.[5] The study found that flights with a first-class or business-class cabin and a separate economy-class section are more likely to report incidents of air rage than flights with only one class of seats.

The study also showed that when flights board from the rear of the aircraft (rather than inviting first-class passengers aboard first), there were fewer incidences of unruly behavior. When people walk past passengers in the first-class or business class cabin and see them swilling their champagne and eating caviar, they feel as if they have been treated unequally and unjustly (even if only at a subconscious level), so they are more prone to losing control and acting rudely or violently.

While we may not react with violence (like Saul or the capuchin monkeys or an angry fellow passenger), we have all compared ourselves to others, and when we nurse envy, our sense of peace and our capacity to respond to situations with poise and self-control are compromised.

So how do we overcome our innate tendency to compare ourselves with others and nurse envy, which fuels shame?

Resist Comparison

First, we can actively and intentionally seek to resist comparison.

Some years ago, I was training for a triathlon when an athletic trainer in our faith community approached me and said, "Such-and-such a pastor is also planning to compete in the triathlon, and you need to beat him." (This pastor leads a growing church in our area that is seen by some parishioners as a competitor to our own.) I said, "It's not about that, but, umm, do you know what his personal best times are?" As it turned out, my trainer friend (who knows I'm a very competitive person by nature) was joking!

The Enneagram is a personality inventory with nine different "types." I happen to be a "3," which is sometimes referred to as the "achiever." I love to win and to be seen as a winner, but as I seek to grow, I am intentionally trying to eschew self-centered comparisons when I compete, as they are driven by my image-conscious and image-constructing false self.

Jonathan Haidt, a social psychologist and professor at NYU's school of business, says that when people stay away from social media, they tend to become more content because they compare themselves with others less.[6] In our technological age, most of us cannot just get off the grid, but we can resist the temptation to compare ourselves with others by limiting screen time or completely eliminating or decreasing our use of social media. I still use one social media platform, Twitter, because my publisher wants readers to be able to interact with me, but other than posting an occasional tweet, I am intentionally resisting the pull of social media.

There Are "None to Be Envied"

Samuel Johnson, an eighteenth-century British scholar, compiled the original English dictionary, and while doing so defined 42,000 words! Johnson had a vivid imagination, which helped him come up with all those definitions, but it also caused him to make detailed and envious comparisons with his rivals. Completely miserable, Johnson devised a strategy to beat envy by trying to convince himself that he was superior to everyone else. But his strategy failed—he was still envious and miserable.

After committing his life to God, Johnson eventually came to believe that love was the only strategy. He wrote that the world is so bursting with sin and sorrow that "there are none to be envied." Everyone has some deep trouble in their own lives or in the life of someone close to them, and so no one should be envied.[7]

> *Everyone has some deep trouble in their own lives or in the life of someone close to them, and so no one should be envied.*

In my vocation as a pastor, I have the privilege of seeing a bit more deeply into people's life circumstances, so I am not surprised by Samuel Johnson's insight. There are many people whose lives appear to be going well on the outside, but almost everyone carries some kind of sorrow.

Some may struggle with anxiety and depression. Some may be in a difficult relationship with a parent or a family member. Some may have lost a parent or other family member prematurely. Some may feel unworthy or have confusion about their identity.

Several years ago, I was following the rise of a well-known and successful pastor who was also a prolific and best-selling author. I envied his ability to be so creative and productive. Sometime later, we happened to be at an event together, and over time we became friends. As I've gotten to know him, I have experienced his kindness, and I also have become privy to an area of suffering in his life that isn't widely known. My envy is gone.

Or consider Elon Musk, one of the most successful and wealthy entrepreneurs in the world, who started Tesla and SpaceX, a company that creates rockets, and acquired Twitter. Because of his success and wealth, he's envied by many. Not long ago, I came across an interview where he described how he was a very small child, a late bloomer, and was terribly bullied and physically beaten up by the mean boys at school. Tearing up, he said, "My father was an evil man. He's done every imaginable evil thing." He said his father had been both physically violent and emotionally abusive. In another interview, he described the stress of running a car company and said that his mind is a "never-ending explosion." I don't know Elon Musk personally, but I have learned enough about his life to know that he is not to be envied.

Samuel Johnson also observed that many successful people cannot truly enjoy their successes. If you are goal-oriented and have a "Type-A" personality, you already know that it is difficult for you to enjoy your successes, because once you achieve a goal, you become so preoccupied with your *next* goal that you don't stop to savor your current success. You don't relish the present moment because you're thinking ahead to the next thing—and then the next thing.

As noted earlier, successful people also struggle to enjoy their successes because they are always comparing themselves to those who are even more successful. Growing up, I had a friend who was a very good hockey player. He went on to play at the Junior A level, which is just below the NHL, but he had friends and acquaintances who made it to the NHL. Compared to me, he was a superstar, but compared to them, he felt mediocre. He couldn't stop comparing himself with the hockey players who had made it into the big leagues, and so he felt like a hack.

Love Does Not Envy

We can also overcome our impulse to envy others by seeking to become a channel of God's love. In 1 Corinthians 13, a beautifully poetic definition of love, the apostle Paul says clearly: "love is patient, love is kind, [and] *it does not envy*" (1 Corinthians 13:4, emphasis mine). Note the importance of envy here as a direct enemy of love. The single most important intention in my life is to grow into a person of love—to grow in patience, to grow in kindness, to refuse to envy. So during my morning times of prayerful meditation, I have been reflecting on 1 Corinthians 13 and reciting the entire chapter as a prayer, expressing the kind of person I hope to become with God's help:

Love is patient, love is kind. It does not envy, it does not boast, it is not proud. It does not dishonor others, it is not self-seeking, it is not easily angered, it keeps no record of wrongs. Love does not delight in evil but rejoices with the truth. It always protects, always trusts, always hopes, always perseveres. (1 Corinthians 13:4–7)

God is using this passage from Scripture to reweave my soul and rewire my mind. I am discovering the truth of Daniel Siegel's words (quoted in chapter 5): "Where our attention goes, neural firing flows, and neural connection grows."

But how does love help us overcome envy?

When we love others, we rejoice with those who rejoice, rather than envying them, and weep with those who weep, rather than gloating over their suffering (Romans 12:15).

In my pastoral work, I have observed spouses who envy each other, who see their partner as a rival, jealously not wanting them to have something good. Though I'm a competitive person by nature, I don't envy my wife when something good happens to her. She's now enrolled in a spiritual formation course and is spiritually flourishing, and I am happy for her. If she were invited to take a vacation to Australia without me and got to snorkel the Great Barrier Reef and see all kinds of dazzling tropical fish . . . well, come to think of it, I would envy her!

I also know people who are envious of their children. If their child is poised to accomplish more or surpass the parent in some way, the parent feels threatened and diminished. But if we really love our children, we won't envy them. Instead, we will rejoice when they are flourishing and weep when they are suffering.

If you truly love someone and something good happens to them, you won't envy them, for you cannot feel both love *and* envy at the same time.

If we envy someone who is a rival or someone we don't know well, we can foster love for them by *acting* in love toward them and praying for them.

When I am tempted to envy someone—such as fellow pastors who are more productive than I am or receive more attention and recognition—I make it a point to remind myself that we're on the same team and then pray God's blessing on them. This is not my first thought, but a conscious, willful decision. When possible, I will try to affirm or help them in some way. Conversely, if I covet someone's life who appears to have a quieter, more private, and less demanding existence than I do, I will pray for that person as well.

Dietrich Bonhoeffer, a German Lutheran pastor, writes that the most significant thing we can do for those whom we might naturally resent is to pray for them. In his classic *Life Together*, he says, "I can no longer condemn or hate a brother [or sister] for whom I pray, no matter how much trouble he [or she] causes me. His [or her] face, that hitherto may have been strange and intolerable, to me is transformed in intercession into the countenance of a brother [or sister] for whom Christ died."[8]

As we've observed in the opening chapters, we can overcome the sense that we are not enough by deeply experiencing God's love. We can pray with the apostle Paul that the eyes of our heart would be enlightened so we would know how wide and long and high and deep is God's love for us in Christ Jesus—for when we know the love of Christ that surpasses knowledge, we will be filled with the fullness of God (Ephesians 3:18–19).

What's more, knowing that we are loved by God will also help us conquer envy. Paul affirmed in 1 Corinthians that love and envy are completely incompatible. When we trust God's love and become a channel of his love, our envy is vanquished.

Gratitude and Joy

We can also overcome our feelings of envy and the shame that accompanies it by embracing practices that nurture gratitude and joy.

When we express gratitude for who we are and what we have been given, our feelings of discontented jealousy of other people and envy about what others have get flushed out of us. As Alex Korb, a neuroscientist at UCLA, observes, we can *experience* mixed emotions, but we cannot focus on both positive and negative feelings at the same time.[9]

> *We can experience mixed emotions, but we cannot focus on both positive and negative feelings at the same time.*
>
> *You cannot feel both love and envy at the same time.*

Right now, take a moment and try to feel both grateful and envious at the same time—it's not possible! Because when we are truly grateful, we will experience joy—and like oil and water, joy and envy are incompatible.

Psychologists tell us that human beings have a "set point" of happiness. A set point of happiness is like an air-conditioning system that has been set to a certain temperature, such as 70°F (21°C). If the sun begins to stream through the window, the temperature inside may rise above 70°F, but will eventually come back to the set point of 70°F. Or, if there is a snowstorm, the temperature may drop below 70°F for a time, but it will eventually return to that "set point" temperature. By nature, some people are more cheerful, while others tend to be gloomier. According to psychologists, about half of our happiness seems to be based on our personal "set point." External circumstances account for another 10 percent, but an amazing 40 percent of our happiness is determined by intentional activity.

One of the most fruitful intentional activities that can boost our happiness and sense of contentment is the practice of giving thanks. Neuroscientists tell us that when we take time to savor a good experience for thirty seconds, the feel-good chemicals serotonin and dopamine are released in our brain. So giving thanks literally changes the chemistry in our brain and makes us feel better.

Each evening, I practice a prayer exercise called "Reimagining the Examen,"[10] which invites me to look back over the last twenty-four hours or so and identify two or three gifts from the day and then offer thanks to God for them. If I were to do the Examen right now, I would give thanks for the really delicious lunch we had yesterday. Our neighbor is a French chef—how fortunate is that?—who started a Michelin-starred restaurant in Vancouver, and he gave us some quince jelly he had made. Quince is a fruit that looks like a cross between a pear and an apple. Some believe it was the forbidden fruit of the garden of Eden! I obviously can't verify that, but we enjoyed this jelly with toast at lunch yesterday.

Then after lunch, it was crisp and clear outside, and I thought it would be a great time to rake leaves with our twelve-year-old son, Joey. We raked leaves together and then went for a run. The work and run on this cool autumn day felt really great—at least for me!

Then last night, I went to our church for an evening presentation about a recent mission trip that our youth took to Cambodia. I was so thankful to hear stories about how these youth were challenged and shaped by their experience. I left feeling deeply grateful that we are able to support several missions in Cambodia that advocate for children, women, and men who are vulnerable to being trafficked as slaves. I was also encouraged to hear accounts of these vulnerable Cambodians finding freedom from slavery and spiritual healing through the love of Christ.

After expressing thanks for each of these gifts, I would zero in on one thing that I feel especially grateful for and hold it in my heart.

After holding that gratitude in my heart, I would imagine myself turning to the Lord and saying, "Thank you, Lord, for my time raking and running with Joey yesterday. Thank you, Lord, for my time raking and running with Joey. Thank you, Lord, for my time with Joey. Amen."

When we associate our good experiences as gifts from a God who loves us, we become less envious and grow more content. Though we will continue to face challenges in our lives, as we trust God's love for us, we will begin to see any gifts we receive as provisions from his loving hands.

Nothing dramatic needs to change in the circumstances of our life for us to experience deep gratitude.

John Ortberg, a respected pastor, served for many years at a church in the San Francisco Bay area. John's best friend, Chuck, is a medical doctor who was diagnosed with cancer. After going through chemotherapy and radiation, he went to the hospital for his first follow-up visit, and the lab results showed that the cancer was just as bad as it had been before the treatments. Chuck knew he was about to die and told John this was the worst day of his life.

But the next morning someone from the hospital called Chuck and said, "We're terribly sorry, but we made a mistake. Yesterday we showed you the wrong lab tests—we showed you the scans of another patient who has not even started treatment yet. You are actually cancer-free. Do you want us to call the lab technician in so you can yell at him?" Chuck said, "Yell at him? I want to kiss him."

He told John that *this* day was the very best day of his life.

Nothing in Chuck's world had actually changed. He didn't win the lottery. He didn't get promoted. He didn't move into a big, fancy new house. But he got another day to do the same things he had done every other day: the same old work, same old house, same old family, same old spouse. Chuck had experienced a shift Anthony de Mello, an Indian Jesuit, describes: "Nothing has changed but my attitude, therefore, everything has changed."[11]

Envy and shame bring nothing good into our lives. They are hissing coals that cause us to seethe in torment. The way to overcome feelings of envy and shame is not to convince ourselves (as Samuel Johnson tried to do) that we are superior to everyone else, or to repeat mantras, saying to ourselves, "I am the greatest. I am the greatest. I am the greatest." Ironically, research shows that people who use such mantras end up feeling worse.[12]

The answer is to look to the Lord.

The psalmist prays, "Those who look to [the LORD] are radiant; their faces are never covered with shame" (Psalm 34:5). When we look to the Lord and experience his love, we become radiant as we channel his love to others and offer love back to God through thanksgiving. When we look to the Lord and experience his love, our faces will never be covered with shame.

Prayer Exercise

Take a deep breath, inhaling and exhaling through your nose. Close your eyes if it helps you to relax. Focus on your breathing as you take several more deep breaths.

Take a moment to reflect on the past twenty-four hours or so. Now recall two or three things for which you feel grateful—an unexpected gift of a moment, an uplifting interaction with someone, a word of affirmation you received, something you saw, heard, smelled, tasted, or felt that moved you with a flicker of delight, or a new opportunity that opened up for you.

Now focus on one of those gifts and hold it in your heart. After a moment, picture yourself turning toward the Lord and say, "Thank you, Lord, for _____. Thank you, Lord, for _____. Thank you, Lord, for _____. Amen."

I encourage you to practice giving thanks to God once a day for the next few weeks and see how it expands your heart and empowers you to resist comparing yourself with others.

Reflection

When we know we are deeply loved by God, we no longer need to fear rejection—the root of shame—because God's "perfect love drives out fear" (1 John 4:18).

Study Guide Questions

1. Who (or what kind of person) do you tend to envy?
2. How can you resist comparing yourself with others?
3. How might becoming a channel of God's love help you overcome envy? How might praying for someone or blessing someone else help you vanquish envy?
4. What is the relationship between practicing gratitude and experiencing freedom from envy? Is there a posture or practice you feel stirred to embrace to help you overcome envy?

Chapter 7

EMBRACING OUR LIMITS

Give me humility in which alone is rest.
—THOMAS MERTON

When I was in high school, I enjoyed competitive team sports. One year, I was the starting quarterback on the football team. I felt like I needed all the help I could get, so I read a book on quarterbacking by Joe Theismann, a former professional player. Like me, he was an undersized, skinny kid in high school. During his first year of college, he sat on the bench and was not even considered a contender for the starting quarterback position. But he worked hard, became the starter, and eventually turned pro. He made the assertion in his book that if you have some talent for football and work hard, you can become a successful pro.

Despite his optimistic words, I knew that was an unlikely path for me. There are a lot of young people who have a reasonable level of athletic ability, but even with hard work, most will not become pro football, basketball, hockey, or baseball players. Professional football was not going to be part of my future.

Growing up, perhaps your parents or someone significant in your life told you, "If you work hard enough, you can become anything you want to be." While that is an exciting message, and it's important to have a growth mindset,[1] it is simply not true that if you work really hard, you can achieve anything you want. No matter how hard we train, most of us will not be running a mile in under three minutes, discovering a cure for cancer, or designing a self-sustaining farm on Mars. Part of the danger of being told you can accomplish anything you dream is that if you don't end up being particularly successful in a worldly sense, you might feel like a failure. Many young people struggle with this fear, which can become paralyzing and even cause them to stop trying. Some feel it's better to be nonchalant than "try hard"; better to aim low rather than risk failure.

Not long ago, I had a conversation with two college students, Kristin and Joshua, who were part of an elite circle at their university. Their academic achievement and leadership potential landed both of them scholarships and the opportunity to receive mentoring from the president of the university. They were both bright, keen, and talented, but when I asked Kristin about her greatest fear, she said she was afraid of not *accomplishing* enough. When I posed the same question to Joshua, he talked about his fear of not *being* enough, of not being liked or accepted by others.

Many young people feel enormous pressure to achieve, and people of all ages continue to carry this weight into their futures.

If you're reading this book, you probably don't live by the slogan "He or she who dies with the most toys wins." But perhaps at some level you believe "He or she who dies with the most accomplishments wins." The pursuit of unlimited achievements may sound like freedom and bliss, but is it really so?

In Christopher Marlowe's play *The Tragical History of Doctor Faustus*, Faustus longs to possess "all Nature's treasury," to "Ransack the ocean . . . and search all corners of the new-found world . . ."[2] To satisfy his hunger for power, he gives his soul to Lucifer in exchange for the services of the junior-devil, Mephistophilis. When Faustus asks Mephistophilis about hell, the junior-devil replies, "Hell hath no limits."[3] There is a real truth hidden in this short definition of hell. While a life without limits may sound like freedom, it may in fact be a tortuous abyss, an existence of perpetual restlessness, endlessly wondering if we have done enough. Rather than holding us back, limits can actually foster and enable our freedom, supporting us so we can fulfill our potential and protecting us from unnecessary failure and shame.

The Freedom of Limits

In *Essentialism: The Disciplined Pursuit of Less*, Greg McKeowen gives an example of an elementary school that was built next to a busy road. He says that at recess the children only played on a small patch of the playground, close to the building, where the grown-ups could keep an eye on them. But then the school built a fence around the playground, and the children began to play everywhere on the playground. The "limits" of the fence provided them with greater freedom. Their freedom, in effect, more than doubled.[4]

Similarly, a painting, however large, is bound by a frame or a wall. A playwright or filmmaker must consider the audience's capacity to sit still and pay attention. A poem is confined to the limits of its literary form. A novel must begin and end within the limits of memory. As the farmer and poet Wendell Berry observes, "The arts characteristically impose limits that are artificial: the five acts of a play, or the fourteen lines of a sonnet. Within these limits artists achieve elaborations of pattern, of sustaining relationships of parts with one another and with the whole, that may be astonishingly complex."[5]

A truly great life also embraces limits. Jesus, as God in human flesh, could have chosen a limitless existence, and yet he chose to limit himself. As a newborn baby, the living God of the universe could not feed himself. He had to learn to breastfeed. At about age one, he—whom Scripture describes as the Word—learned to speak his first word. As a toddler, he fell and scraped his knees as he learned to walk. As an apprentice carpenter, he got splinters in his fingers, and as he learned to use a hammer, he would sometimes miss the nail and strike his thumb. While he likely didn't curse uttering his given name, he would have yelled in pain! We also know from the Gospels that Jesus grew hungry, thirsty, and tired, and he could only be in one place at a time.

In fact, Jesus never traveled beyond the confines of a relatively small region in ancient Palestine. His life's work was also limited by what he discerned to be his Father's will. During his earthly ministry, Jesus once healed a paralyzed man in Jerusalem by the pool at Bethesda. While there were many people with disabilities who lay near the pool—especially those who were blind and paralyzed (John 5:2–3)—Jesus only restored one person. Why did Jesus heal only one person? He later explains, "I tell you the truth, the Son can do nothing by himself. He does only what he sees the Father doing. Whatever the Father does, the Son also does" (John 5:19 NLT).

Jesus constrained himself by willingly doing *only* what his Father had called him to do.

While Jesus was compassionate, he wasn't always driven by the seemingly obvious need of the moment. When Jesus's good friend Lazarus was in critical condition, his sisters Mary and Martha sent an urgent message to Jesus, saying, "Lord, the one you love is sick" (John 11:3). Their intention was to make Jesus feel obligated to come quickly, but Jesus didn't rush to Lazarus. Instead, after receiving the message, he stayed where he was for two more days.

By the time Jesus finally arrived at Mary and Martha's home, Lazarus had already died and been buried. Disappointed that Jesus had arrived four days too late, Martha said, "Lord, if you had been here, my brother would not have died" (John 11:21). Jesus's love for Lazarus and the desperate plea of his two sisters did not dictate Jesus's agenda. Rather, he was guided by the voice of his Father. In sync with God's timing, Jesus went to Lazarus's tomb and raised him from the dead.[6]

The greatest human being who ever lived didn't strive to cram as much as possible into his short lifetime of roughly thirty-three years. Jesus let his life be limited by God's will— *and* liberated by God's will.

Discerning Our Limits

As we trace the footsteps of Jesus and seek the Father's will, we will discover both our limits and the liberation that accepting those limits brings. Many of us live with the feeling of perpetual overload. There may be extraordinary situations when we have to carry an unusually heavy weight for a season—raising young children, going through rotations as a medical school student, needing to juggle a few different jobs just to make ends meet. Yet when our lives feel perpetually pressed down by the weight of too many demands, it is often the result of having overly porous boundaries.

We can find greater freedom when we realize that we're not called to meet every single need.

Parker Palmer, a wise Quaker elder, describes how he came to this realization. In his beautiful book *Let Your Life Speak*, he writes, "If I try to be or do something noble that has nothing to do with who I am, I may look good to others and to myself for a while. But the fact that I am exceeding my limits will eventually have consequences. I will distort myself, the other, and our relationship—and may end up doing more damage than if I had never set out to do this particular 'good.'"[7]

Palmer gives a personal example:

Over the years, I have met people who have made a very human claim on me by making known their need to be loved. For a long time, my response was instant and reflexive, born of the "oughts" I had absorbed: "Of course you need to be loved. Everyone does. And I love you."

It took me a long time to understand that although everyone needs to be loved, I cannot be the source of that gift to everyone who asks me for it. There are some relations in which I am capable of love and others in which I am not. To pretend otherwise, to put out promissory notes I am unable to honor, is to damage my own integrity and that of the person in need—all in the name of love.[8]

Realizing we do not have to say yes to every noble or good opportunity can feel as if a heavy load has been lifted. By discerning our limits, we can actually care for ourselves—and then we can offer the gift of ourselves to others.

I know this dynamic personally. By nature, I feel compelled to try to accomplish as much as possible, not necessarily out of an altruistic desire to contribute, but largely to please and impress others, shore up my self-esteem, and validate my existence.

Part of my restless over-functioning, along with the accompanying shame from the niggling feeling that I haven't done enough, stems from not having discerned God's will and not recognizing that God is giving me freedom to say "no." I find myself praying with Thomas Merton, "Free me from laziness that goes about disguised as activity when activity is not required of me. . . . Give me humility in which alone is rest."[9] Increasingly, I long to eschew the vain glory and futility of trying to impress others and live more consciously before the eyes of God.

If we live more consciously before the loving gaze of God, we will receive insight into God's providential limits for our lives. When we accept these limits as a gift from God, we can live with less shame and false guilt—feelings that stem from a sense that we haven't done quite enough—and discover more joyful contentment.

> *"Free me from laziness that goes about disguised as activity when activity is not required of me. . . . Give me humility in which alone is rest."*
> —Thomas Merton

When I made the transition from the corporate world to vocational Christian ministry, I enrolled in the Arrow Leadership Program, a ministry that helps develop young, emerging

Christian leaders. During our graduation ceremony, Leighton Ford, the founder of this ministry, prayed a public blessing over each of the graduates. Though that was more than twenty-five years ago now, I still vividly remember him praying that I would be given a ministry in Canada and Japan.

At the time Leighton prayed this blessing over me, I was studying at a theological seminary in the Boston area and would soon head west to help start a new church in southern California. But a couple of years later, God called me to Canada, where I have now served for more than two decades, and also unexpectedly opened up an opportunity for me to minister in Japan. Given the religious demographics of Vancouver and Japan and my own gift limitations, I realize that I will not be leading huge ministries. There is a limit to my call, and I accept this limit—and in this limitation, I find freedom.

Sometimes we discover our limitations as someone prays prophetically over us or as we follow the unfolding of God's providential plan. Other times, we may discover our limitations through some feedback or observation we make about ourselves. I've long known that I won't make any contributions to the world through music or singing. This has been confirmed when occasionally, during worship at church, someone beside me has asked, "Are you trying to sing harmony?" (meaning instead of the melody), when I was simply singing off tune!

Our life stage also can represent a season of limitation. If you're a mother or father of young children, caring for aging parents, experiencing the loss of an important relationship, starting a new line of work with a steep learning curve, facing a health challenge or financial setback, or needing to work two or three jobs just to pay the rent, you will experience significant limitations.

We can also discover our limits by discerning whether an activity feels life-giving or draining. Parker Palmer writes, "One sign that I am violating my own nature in the name of nobility is a condition called burnout. Though usually regarded as the result of trying to give too much, burnout in my experience results from trying to give what I do not possess—the ultimate in giving too little! Burnout is a state of emptiness, to be sure, but it does not result from giving all I have: it merely reveals the nothingness from which I was trying to give in the first place."[10]

Trying to give what we do not have is surely a road to burnout. However, the opposite can also be true—attempting to do too much of something we actually enjoy can also feel burdensome. When I was a new pastor, I often felt a sense of delight if I looked at my calendar and saw that I would be meeting multiple people over the course of the day. But I soon discovered that if I had seven or more pastoral care meetings in a single day, I would feel exhausted. Even if we find inherent joy in something, as the saying goes, "too much of a good thing becomes a bad thing." We need limits, even with the good things in our life.

This process of discerning what imparts life and what drains us, when to say no and when to say yes, involves trial and error. There will be times when we may say no, but in retrospect realize that we were feeling intimidated, afraid, or depressed and so regret not saying yes. In other cases, we may have said yes, and later realize we should have said no.

Other times, we will be torn between two options, and neither promises short-term satisfaction. In such cases, Gabor Maté, a Vancouver-based physician and author, says, "If you face the choice between feeling guilt and resentment, choose the guilt every time. . . . If a refusal saddles you with guilt, while consent leaves you with resentment in its wake, opt for the guilt. Resentment is soul suicide."[11]

As we seek to discern how to decide, it can be helpful to draw on the wisdom of Saint Ignatius of Loyola. He counsels us to imagine making a particular choice and then to prayerfully discern whether one path gives us a sense of peace and draws us into greater sync with God's Spirit, or if one scenario leaves us feeling restless, listless, and disconnected from God's Spirit.[12]

> *"If a refusal saddles you with guilt, while consent leaves you with resentment in its wake, opt for the guilt. Resentment is soul suicide."*
> —Gabor Maté

If we desire to follow God, a growing sense of inner peace and joy will tend to accompany the choices we make that are consistent with his will.

When we are facing an important decision that does not need immediate clarity, we can ideally take at least several days for prayerful discernment. Otherwise, if we are asked to do something early in the morning or late in the afternoon, or if our favorite sports team won or lost, our mood in the moment may predispose us toward a choice we may later regret.

It is also helpful to imagine how we might counsel someone else to make the same decision if he or she were in our situation. For example, I was once asked to make a statement about a controversial issue. While I aligned myself on a particular side of this issue, there were many thoughtful people who took the opposite position. By nature, I don't mind "stepping into the arena," even if it means getting pushback, but as I imagined counseling someone *else* in the same situation, I saw myself saying, "Given your role, by coming down publicly on one side of this issue, you will further polarize people in the community." So I decided to decline the invitation.

When facing a big decision, the Jesuits, who are trained in spiritual discernment, encourage us to imagine ourselves standing before God at the end of our life and giving an account of our decision. For example, let's say you envision yourself accepting a new job with a higher salary, but you know you will not be able to see much of your family. As you imagine yourself standing before God, you might feel regret over that decision.[13]

Even after we set aside time to reflect and pray, we may still feel completely torn between two options. As we learn when to say yes and when to say no, we need to offer ourselves the same kindness, patience, and grace we would show to a good friend.[14]

Redefining Success

A publisher once asked Thomas Merton—a well-known monk and the author of the critically acclaimed, bestselling memoir *The Seven Storey Mountain*—to write something about "the Secret of Success." Merton refused. Instead he wrote, "If I had a message to my contemporaries, it was surely this: Be anything you like, be madmen, drunks, and bastards of every shape and form, but at all costs avoid one thing: success. If you have learned only how to be a success, your life has probably been wasted."[15]

If our primary pursuit is success, we will forget to *live*, we will fail to enjoy life, and we will lose sight of God and what matters most.

When I became the pastor of my church in Vancouver, the congregation had cycled through twenty ministers in twenty years and had declined from over 1,000 congregants to a little over 100 over the course of a couple of decades. As those who are familiar with my work know, during my first or second week on the job, the secretary walked into my office and said, "If the ship sinks now, everyone will blame you because you were the last captain at the helm." I felt enormous pressure to generate momentum and harbored a restless energy to deliver. A large part of my motivation to work hard was driven by my desire to avoid the shame of failure.

But during this season, a verse from Scripture came to my spirit, "[God says] I will raise up for myself a faithful priest, who will do according to what is in my heart and mind" (1 Samuel 2:35). As I reflected on this verse, I was reassured that my calling as a pastor—and as a human being—was to discern the mind and heart of God, who is loving, wise, and generous. You will be truly successful when you seek to do the Father's will. As you grow in your knowledge of God's will for your life, you will be set free from the bondage of fear and shame. When you know God's most important priorities for your life, you also will be able to set limits so you can protect what matters most.

The late Clay Christensen, who was a Harvard Business School professor and the author of *The Innovator's Dilemma*, described an experience he had when he was working for a management consulting firm. When one of the partners told him he needed to come in on a Saturday to help on a project, Clay responded, "Oh, I am sorry. I have made a commitment that every Saturday is a day to be with my wife and children." The partner, displeased, stormed off, but later returned and said, "Clay, fine. I've talked with everyone on the team, and they said they will come in on Sunday instead. So I expect you to be there." Clay sighed and said, "I appreciate you trying to do that. But Sunday will not work. I have given Sunday to God, so I won't be able to come in." Realizing what is truly essential helps us set healthy boundaries, emboldening us to say a confident no to our secondary priorities and a robust yes to our primary priorities.[16]

Our world tends to glamorize what is big and public, as reflected in the popular saying "Go big or go home." But when we increasingly see our work as the fulfillment of God's will, and we tend to that work in his presence, even the seemingly small and obscure tasks will feel noble.

In the wonderful book *A Theology of the Ordinary*, Julie Canlis points out that when Moses was penning the creation poem in Genesis 1, he counted off the six days of creation. As people in his ancient world of Mesopotamia heard this story for the first time, they would have been counting in their heads, "one, two, three, four, five, six." They would have sat up and asked, "What is built in six days?" (or six symbolic time periods in their world). "A temple!" The six days of creation expressed in the poetry of the creation story lead to the question, "What is God building through the earth?" A temple! If, in fact, the whole earth is the true temple, the earth itself takes on supreme significance as a place to worship God. Ordinary life on earth, including our ordinary daily work, *is* our worship.[17]

What we do may not be big and public, but if we are living in the will of God, we are doing something noble. Our work *is* worship.

As a young person, Dave Hataj assumed that the most noble, God-pleasing vocation would be to serve either as a pastor or a missionary. After earning a doctoral degree in theology, he served on the pastoral staff of a large church in California. But after a time—and to his surprise and dismay—he sensed God leading him to assume a management role in his parents' family-owned manufacturing business in rural Wisconsin. He did not really want to work in that oily, grimy machine shop! Pornography was strewn everywhere, and beer was so much part of the culture that his father had put a quarter-barrel keg in the lunchroom for the employees. Even though the company only had seventeen employees, they were divided into warring factions that constantly tried to sabotage each other.

Though this environment was challenging, Dave believed that the workplace is one of the primary places we are shaped spiritually, since we spend most of our waking hours there each week. Although he did not proselytize at work, he saw himself as a pastor. As he shared honestly about his past with alcoholism, he demonstrated vulnerability and genuine care for his team, and they began to open up to him about their issues. These relationships prompted Dave to offer financial support to any staff who wanted to receive counseling.

Inspired by Jesus, who spent most of his working life as a blue-collar craftsman, Dave began to cast a vision of the noble task of making quality gears, sprockets, and pulleys. Although changing the corporate culture felt excruciatingly slow and was often discouraging, Dave—who has now been leading the business for more than thirty years—now sees that the growing trust, mutual respect, and commitment to quality craftsmanship in his company reflects the character and values of Jesus.[18]

No matter how mundane our day-to-day work might seem, when we work with and for God in the temple of the earth, everything we do is our worship. Although our work may not be particularly glamorous or widely known, if we are living in the will of God, whatever we do matters. Our calling may involve working in obscurity and without high pay, raising children, staying faithful in a marriage that is challenging, or keeping a home in decent order.[19] Though these tasks might seem unremarkable to us, they are *seen* and valued by God. In fact, according to Jesus, if your work for God is behind the scenes and unnoticed, God takes special notice (Matthew 6:1–18). The apostle Paul also writes that these hidden parts of our community should be regarded with special honor (1 Corinthians 12:23).

We tend to regard those who are making a killing financially or who have gained widespread recognition as great, but there are countless truly great people whose names you have never heard. My friend Ray is neither wealthy nor famous. He has never held a prestigious, highly paying job, but he worked hard, raised a family, lived generously, and loved people well while quietly helping refugees from Ethiopia and Iran get settled into homes in his Canadian city.

On the occasion of his official retirement, a journalist in his town wrote:

> I've met many amazing people in my more than 34 years in journalism—people who have risen to the pinnacle of their chosen fields—award-winning academics, authors, politicians, inventors, business leaders, actors, rock stars, Olympians, professional athletes, adventurers and humanitarians. But the greatest person I know and have ever met . . . is Ray Matheson."[20]

You don't have to be well known or wealthy, and you don't have to do something widely regarded as heroic to be truly great. But you must live *your life*, not someone else's.

Henri Nouwen, a wonderfully perceptive priest and author, wrote, "No two lives are the same. We often compare our lives with those of others, trying to decide whether we are better or worse off, but such comparisons do not help us much. We have to live our life, not someone else's. We have to hold *our own* cup. We have to dare to say: 'This is my life, the life that is given to me, and it is this life that I have to live, as well as I can.'"[21] Led by the Spirit as you discover your unique path, you will live a truly beautiful life—and *no one* but *you* can live it.

As you embrace both the limits and the potential of your calling, you will grow into your true and glorious self, and that's nothing to be ashamed of.

Prayer Exercise

---◆---

I pray the following "welcoming prayer" (I alluded to it in chapter 5)[22] as part of my morning meditation, inviting the Spirit to help deliver me from my inclination to pursue esteem, influence, or success. I also pray this simple prayer throughout the day, whenever I feel an unhealthy desire to compare myself with others or to seek validation, control, or security.

Breathe deeply in and out of your nose several times while imagining yourself resting before the loving gaze of God.

As you inhale, pray, *I consent to the work of the Holy Spirit.*

As you exhale, pray, *I let go of my desire for affection and esteem.*

Inhale. Exhale, *I let go of my desire for power and control.*

Inhale. Exhale, *I let go of my desire for security and survival.*

Reflection

When I exceed my limits, I will distort myself and others, and I will also distort my relationship with God.

Take a moment to reflect on the limits in your life right now. Are there any areas where you might be trying to give from "nothingness" instead of the fullness of who God made you to be? Invite the Spirit to help you hold *your own cup* so you can live the life you have been given.

Study Guide Questions

1. Rather than believing that if you work hard enough, you can become anything you want, how might recognizing your limits foster a sense of freedom for you? How does exceeding your limits damage you and others?

2. How did Jesus choose to *limit* himself during his earthly existence?

3. Practically, what might help you discern the will of God and embrace your limits so you know when to say yes or no to something?

4. How can you ensure that you live your life, not someone else's?

Chapter 8

FULFILLING OUR POTENTIAL

*Like humility, generosity comes from seeing that
everything we have and everything we accomplish
comes from God's grace and God's love for us . . .*[1]
—DESMOND TUTU

My friend Peter Ash was born with albinism, a rare genetic condition characterized by the absence of pigment in the skin, hair, and eyes. He is also partially blind. Growing up, Peter lived in a poor, working-class neighborhood in Montréal, and he would take public transit everywhere. Whenever he got on a bus, people would whisper, "Hey, look at that albino over there." Kids at school would call him Casper the Friendly Ghost or Frosty the Snowman. To read the small print of a textbook, he would have to hold it against his nose, and his classmates would gawk at him. As a young person, Peter's secret fantasy was to be like all the other kids in his school.

When Peter was eight years old, on a sunny July day, he was walking through the alley behind the apartment building where he lived and noticed an old bike. He had never been taught how to ride a bike, but he decided to give it a try. Holding the bike steady, he slid onto the seat and then started wobbling down the alley, picking up speed. Suddenly, his front tire hit a pothole, and the bike catapulted him into the air. As his body thudded the pavement, he scraped his knee, and it began bleeding.

Looking up toward his family's second-floor apartment, Peter wondered if his mother was still on the balcony, hanging laundry on the clothesline. Time seemed to stand still. "I'm bleeding and I'm waiting," he told me, "and then, all of a sudden, I hear a woman from an apartment on the other side of the alley yell at my mother, 'He's blind! He shouldn't be riding a bike!'"

Humiliated, Peter wondered, "What do I do?" Finally, his mother hollered, "Peter, don't listen to her! Get back on that bike!" Peter got back on the bike and rode smoothly for a couple of minutes before falling again. "My mother changed the course of my life in that moment," Peter said, "because she taught me that nobody else had the power to define me, and the only way to be defeated was by giving up."

Throughout elementary school, Peter struggled with his grades because he could not read anything written on the blackboard. His fifth-grade teacher told him, "You're lazy and you have a bad attitude. You'll never make anything of your life." But remembering his mother's words, "Get back on that bike," he managed to push through elementary school.

During his teenage years, Peter began rebelling and using drugs. Peter's father had been powerfully transformed by his relationship with Christ, so one Sunday he brought Peter to a worship service, where Peter also experienced a life-changing encounter with Jesus.

Throughout high school, Peter's mother helped him see

beyond what others considered to be his weaknesses and failures, things that had always been sources of shame. "Peter," she often told him, "you're not strange or weird—you're unique." As he experienced God's love and grew in his understanding of God's plan for his life, he gradually overcame the shaming put-downs of his childhood peers and the dismissive teachers who said he would never make anything of his life.

In time, Peter went on to earn a master's degree and then served as a pastor for a decade before launching a successful commercial real estate business.

One evening, after coming home from work, Peter came across a BBC article about people with albinism, mostly children, in Tanzania who were being murdered for their body parts, as some people believed that the hand, leg, skin, hair, or eyes of a person with albinism had magical powers that could be used as an instrument of healing for others. This story shook Peter to the core. He flew to Tanzania to conduct his own investigation. As he traveled through the country, he was amazed to see hundreds of people with albinism. (There are about ten times more people per capita with albinism in Tanzania than in North America.)

This experience moved Peter to start a nonprofit organization called Under the Same Sun, which advocates for people with albinism in Tanzania. Eleven years ago, Under the Same Sun started private schools for over 400 children with albinism who otherwise wouldn't have received an education. Many of these students have gone on to university, and some are now working for the government or the private sector. This is significant in Tanzania, as the name for albinism in Swahili is *zeruzeru*, which means "zero zero" or "ghost-like."

After Miriamu, a young girl with albinism, was murdered for her body parts, Under the Same Sun worked with the United Nations to begin a nationwide campaign to teach the public about albinism. As of this writing, people with albinism in Tanzania have not been murdered for their body parts for more than five years.

When we experience God's unconditional love and unequivocal grace, our feelings of shame and not being enough—which sap an enormous amount of our energy—begin to recede. As space opens within us and we begin to embrace our limitations (as discussed in chapter 7), we will discover we have more energy and inner resources to devote to creating goodness and beauty in the world.

Strength in Weakness: Risking Failure

As we embrace our limitations and begin to realize our God-given gifts and potential, we will become less fearful about risking possible failure. Curt Thompson, a psychiatrist and author, says that "Satan uses shame as an emotional weapon against us to prevent us from fulfilling our God-given calling."[2] Similarly, C. S. Lewis contends that shame prevents us from doing good—perhaps even more so than vice.[3] Shame causes us to hold back and impedes the natural flow of God's grace in our lives—and into the world.

One of the core lies that shame whispers is that we have to do something *perfectly*. Albert Camus's novel *The Plague* describes a deadly epidemic that strikes Oran, a city on Africa's Mediterranean coast. Joseph Grand, a clerk for Oran's government, is aspiring to write a novel. His opening sentence is *"One fine morning in the month of May an elegant young horsewoman might have been riding a handsome sorrel mare along the flowery avenues of the Bois de Boulogne."*

But he can't get the sentence exactly right. He obsesses over each word, agonizingly revising just how the horsewoman and

> *Shame causes us to hold back and impedes the natural flow of God's grace in our lives—and into the world.*

her mare might ride down the avenues of Bois de Boulogne. In his perfectionism, Joseph Grand can't get past this first sentence, and so there is never a next sentence—let alone a novel.

If we aim to do something perfectly—whether it's writing a sentence, giving a speech, playing a piece of music, or attempting some other endeavor—we will hesitate and choke. If we finally overcome our inertia and get started, our success or failure will only be about *us* and *our performance*. But if our final goal is to serve God and others rather than our personal achievement or how others view us, we will be freed from our ego—our false self—and have a greater capacity to serve and love. And as we seek to serve and love others, our lives will bear more abundant fruit.

My wife, Sakiko, was raised in Japan, a culture where people are especially self-conscious about how others perceive them. When she worked as an editor and publisher in Japan, she took pride in her ability to express herself in her native (Japanese) language. After moving to Canada to marry me, she felt one of the greatest difficulties of being an immigrant was realizing that her English would never be perfect. A few years ago, she enrolled in a spiritual direction course and is now offering spiritual direction to a handful of Japanese people (in Japan, using Zoom) as well as English-speaking Canadians. If she felt she needed to have perfect English, she would not be able to engage in this ministry with English speakers, but because she knows she is deeply loved by God, she is able to let go of her natural tendency toward perfectionism and joyfully use her gifts to serve others.

In Henri Nouwen's book *Here and Now*, he writes, "It is not 'excelling' but 'serving' that makes us most human."[4] When we encounter the deep love of God, we are freed of our tendency to focus on our self and be preoccupied with our performance and reputation, which liberates us to offer our gifts in service to others.

When I entered high school, my highest priority was to become part of the popular group of "bad-boy" athletes. I worked really hard and was finally accepted in this group, but just barely. I remember being bothered whenever a less popular, less cool kid tried to sit near us in the school cafeteria because I felt like the kid's presence somehow lowered our group status, so I would shoo him away. Of course, it was my immense insecurity that caused me to try so hard to be part of the popular group in the first place, and it also made me try to block others from becoming part of our circle.

> *When we encounter the deep love of God, we are freed of our tendency to focus on our self and be preoccupied with our performance and reputation, which liberates us to offer our gifts in service to others.*

When I came to know Christ, I felt both deeply loved and truly honored by God, though I couldn't have articulated it this way at the time. Because I intuitively felt honored and esteemed by the Maker of the universe, I was no longer as concerned about being part of the "cool" group. When a student from a "lower rung" in the school's social caste started moving toward Christ, I began to spend a lot of time sitting with him in the school cafeteria during lunch hour. Because I felt loved and honored by God, I came to have more confidence and could break free from my self-absorbed pursuit of social status, and eventually I began to care for others.

The Transforming Work
of the Holy Spirit

In the Gospel of John, Jesus stands up on the last day of the Feast of Tabernacles and cries out, "Whoever believes in me, as Scripture has said, rivers of living water will flow from within them" (John 7:38). What did he mean by "rivers of living water"? In the next verse, we learn that these "rivers" refer to the Holy Spirit (John 7:39).

When we begin to follow Jesus Christ, God comes and lives within us by his Spirit. Because it is in God's very nature to pour himself out like a nourishing river for others, serving them in love, we will also long to serve others. Every human being is made in the image of God, so every person has the capacity to serve, but those who have been served directly by Christ are uniquely empowered to serve others. We are called to "lose" our lives so we may "find" them by serving others (Matthew 10:39).

A journalist friend who lives in Asia told me a story about a man named Arjun from India. As a young man, Arjun moved to Mumbai to work as a chef, but then he got mixed up with the wrong crowd and ended up working as a pimp instead. He would go into the lobbies of five-star hotels and invite men to have sexual encounters with women and children. Though he was making a lot of money, he began to feel restless and unfulfilled. One day, for no apparent reason, he walked into a church sanctuary and began praying. This experience inspired a spiritual quest, and he eventually met Jesus. Thanks to the presence of Jesus in his life, Arjun no longer works as a pimp, but is now using his culinary skills to train women who want to leave the sex trade to become professional cooks so they can begin a new way of life. Because of Jesus's presence in his life, Arjun is *serving* women and children instead of exploiting them.

Discovering the Joy of Serving Others

This biblical paradox of "finding" our life by "losing" it (Matthew 10:39) is corroborated by neuroscience. A University of California research project demonstrates that acting generously activates the same reward pathway that is stimulated by sex and food—a correlation that may help to explain why giving and helping feel so good.[5] Moreover, when we love, serve, and give to others, we reflect the character of God, whose essence is to give.

On the night before Jesus went to the cross, he shared a final meal with his students, then pushed himself up from the table, poured water into a basin, and stooped down to wash the feet of his students. "Now that I, your Lord and Teacher, have washed your feet," he said to them, "you also should wash one another's feet. I have set you an example that you should do as I have done for you. . . . Now that you know these things, you will be blessed if you do them" (John 13:14–15, 17). Jesus doesn't say, "Now that you know these things, you will be blessed if you discuss them in your small groups." Instead, he says, "You will be blessed if you *do* them" (emphasis mine).

This experience of blessedness manifests itself as joy—an emotion that shows up quite early in our life. One study has found that toddlers younger than age two exhibited more happiness when giving treats to a puppet than when receiving treats themselves. They were even happier when they gave the puppets treats from their own bowl.[6] A mother of a seven-year-old boy told me her son invited a special needs boy who couldn't speak to come to his home just so they could be in the same room together. The occasion brought joy to her young son, his friend, and the mother.

The joy of giving can also be experienced in old age. Dr. Shigeaki Hinohara, a devout Christian and the son of a pastor, became a renowned physician in Japan and then kept offering medical care to people until he was 105 years old. Yes, that's right, 105 years old!

Earlier in Dr. Hinohara's life, when he was 58 years old, he was on an airplane that was hijacked, and he was taken as a hostage to North Korea. He thought he would die there but was miraculously released, then had such a profound sense of gratitude that he made a commitment to devote the rest of his life to serving others. Along with his medical practice, Dr. Hinohara began to crisscross Japan, speaking to elementary school students, senior citizens, and everyone in between about how to flourish by serving others.

After a number of years, Dr. Hinohara generously volunteered his medical services to his patients, refusing to accept any payment. As soon as he stepped into a room at St. Luke's Hospital in Tokyo, patients would light up and be filled with new hope and energy. Dr. Hinohara beautifully embodied his core message of loving service until he died.

When we encounter the love of God and use our gifts to serve others—whether we're from Japan, India, or elsewhere, whether we're seven or 105 years old, or somewhere in between—we reflect the image of the joyous God of the universe, who *loves* to serve. When we offer our time and gifts to others with the servant heart of Jesus, we will be freed from shame because joy and shame are incompatible. When our heads are no longer bent over in shame, the door concealing our true self begins to open, and we can grow into the beautiful creation God created us to be.

Yet our service doesn't have to be as dramatic as helping people find their way out of the sex trade or as lifesaving as practicing good medicine. We will also be filled with meaning and joy when we serve others through small or mundane acts of love.

For example, I was doing some yard work the other day, and I put our golden retriever, Sasha, on a leash and then looped the end of the leash over a hook on our fence. As I began cutting the grass on the boulevard along the side of our house, a woman I'm acquainted with approached, pushing her cart filled with bottles and cans she collects to generate income for herself. She reached out to pet Sasha, our golden retriever, who promptly rolled over and offered her belly. "Is it OK if I give her some of my soda crackers?" the woman asked. There was a part of me that wanted to say no, as I wondered if that would cut into this woman's own needed food supply, but I also knew that when she gave those soda crackers to Sasha, the pleasure circuits in her brain would light up, and so I agreed. And sure enough, as she shared her food with our dog, she beamed.

Then she looked at our fig tree and asked, "How are your figs doing?"

"They're doing pretty well," I said. "Would you like some?" She was happy to receive some figs—and I was even happier to give her some!

You don't need to be a religious person to know the joy of mirroring God's generosity.

James Doty, a neurosurgeon in California, made a fortune as a medical technology entrepreneur and pledged stock worth $30 million to charity. At the time, his net worth was more than $75 million. But when the stock market crashed, he lost everything and suddenly found himself bankrupt. All he had left was the stock that had been cashed out and pledged to a charity.

His lawyers told him, "Dr. Doty, given your circumstances, everyone will understand if you want to get out of this pledge of $30 million, and you can do it legally." Jim responded, "One of the persistent myths in our society is that money will make you happy. I grew up poor and I thought money would give me everything I did not have—control, power, and love. When I finally had all the money I had ever dreamed of, I discovered that money did not make me happy, and when I lost it all, my false friends disappeared." Jim decided to go ahead with his contribution and said, "At that moment I realized that the only way money can bring happiness is to give it away."[7]

When we give our money, our time, and our energy to

131

others, we glimpse a truth at the center of the universe: "It is more blessed to give than to receive" (Acts 20:35). This truth was perfectly manifested through Jesus, who knew he was deeply beloved and then lived into his full potential by laying down his life for others.

As we overcome our sense of not being enough through an experience of God's gracious and unconditional love, we will discover our gifts as we serve others. Through loving service, we fulfill the larger purpose of our existence and feel a deep sense of joy and fulfillment. As we step into this virtuous cycle of contribution and joy, becoming more like the most joyous Being in the universe as the divine image is restored within us, we become more of our true self.

Prayer Exercise

———◇———

Take several deep breaths, inhaling and exhaling through
your nose.

As you inhale, focus on filling your chest with breath—*Spirit*.

As you exhale, imagine your breath—*Spirit*—flowing into
the world, covering everything in its path with love and grace.

As you inhale, pray: *Fill me with your living water.*

As you exhale, pray: *Flow through me into the world.*

Reflection

Imagine yourself filled to overflowing with the love and grace of
God. Now imagine that spring of living water pouring over the
edge of a limestone cliff—a waterfall, cascading goodness and
beauty into the world. Listen to the sound of the water pound-
ing the rocks and feel the cool spray on your face. If you hear
any shameful whispers of imperfection, picture each whisper as
a pebble and throw it into the rushing water, then imagine the
rushing water flowing into the ocean of God's love.

Now imagine yourself plunging under the waterfall. As the
water pounds against your back and head, imagine it washing
any fears of failure into the ocean of God's grace.

When you feel cleansed, step out of the waterfall and invite
the Spirit to show you someone who is longing to discover this
lifegiving spring; then begin to imagine how you might respond.

Study Guide Questions

1. How does shame prevent us from fulfilling God's calling on our lives?

2. Like Peter's mother, have you ever experienced someone helping you to see beyond what you considered to be your weaknesses and failures?

3. How does God's grace help us overcome our fear of failure so we can take risks? How does experiencing God's love enable us to contribute to the world?

4. How are you being stirred to serve others?

Chapter 9

AWAKENING
TO BEAUTY

Beauty will save the world.
—FYODOR DOSTOYEVSKY

In the movie *The Shawshank Redemption*, Andy Dufresne (played by Tim Robbins) is falsely accused of murder and ends up spending twenty years in prison.

Andy has been assigned to work in the prison library and receives a donation of vinyl records that includes a recording of Mozart's *The Marriage of Figaro*. In an act of defiance, he plays the music over the public loudspeakers, creating a sense of euphoria throughout the prison yard. A fellow inmate, Red (played by Morgan Freeman), provides a voice-over narration for this scene:

> I have no idea to this day what those two Italian ladies were singing about. Truth is, I don't want to know. Some things are best left unsaid. I'd like to think they were singing about something so beautiful it can't be expressed in words, and makes your heart ache because of it.

I tell you, those voices soared higher and farther than anybody in a gray place dares to dream. It was like some beautiful bird flapped into our drab little cage and made those walls dissolve away, and for the briefest of moments, every last man in Shawshank felt free.

Beauty can dissolve the walls that imprison us—including the wall of shame that prevents us from becoming our glorious, true self—and set us free.

Shame involves self-analysis, critique, and condemnation, which are primarily left-brain activities. When we are exposed to beauty, the right hemisphere of our brain becomes more active, and the left hemisphere of our brain, where our analyzing inner critic operates, grows quiet, leaving shame with less room to work.[1]

To study the way different activities affect the brain, researchers at Stanford University sent participants out on a ninety-minute walk. Some hiked the Dish, a scenic trail in the foothills near campus, while others walked along one of the busiest streets in Silicon Valley. Before and after the walk, neuroscientists put participants in an fMRI machine to capture their brain's resting activity and had them answer questions about their state of mind, including how much they agreed with statements such as, "My attention is focused on aspects of myself I wish I'd stop thinking about." After the scenic hike—but not the walk on

> *When we are exposed to beauty, the right hemisphere of our brain becomes more active, and the left hemisphere of our brain, where our analyzing inner critic operates, grows quiet, leaving shame with less room to work.*

the busy roadway—participants reported less anxiety and negative self-focused thinking. Their post-walk brain scans revealed
less activity in the area of the brain linked with self-criticism,
sadness, and depression.[2]

Shame causes us both literally and figuratively to curl in
on our self. But beauty can call us out of our anxious self-
absorption. The French mystic Simone Weil writes that beauty
requires us "to give up our imaginary position as the center."[3]

When we see sunrays breaking through leafy branches in a
forest or glistening orange-gold on the water, or when we smell
the scent of cedar trees or notice the flutter of a hummingbird's
wings or the curl of a squirrel's tail as he nibbles a nut, we can
be drawn out of our preoccupation with ourself as we become
more attuned to the mysterious grace that is woven into the
natural world around us.

I know a woman whose husband has an advanced stage
of cancer. Though she feels deeply sad, angry at God, and
scared about her future, each morning she walks through her
neighborhood to think and pray and enjoy the beautiful homes
and gardens she passes.

On a recent morning, as she was walking through her
neighborhood feeling especially distraught, in tears she
expressed her anger, grief, and fear to God. As she was passing
a house, she noticed a little table in the front of the yard with a
lovely bouquet of oregano flowers and a sign that read, "Please
take this bouquet." She took the bouquet in her hands, brought
it to her face, and felt nourished by the scent. She laughed with
delight, as these flowers seemed to be such a tangible sign of
God's love for her and her husband.

Even when we are preoccupied with our pain, beauty can

draw us out of our self and evoke joy. Though we will continue to feel grief and sorrow, beauty can usher us into the grace and love of God.

Beauty Awakens Us to the Love of God

Several years ago, on a clear, starlit summer night on British Columbia's Sunshine Coast, I was canoeing with my longtime friend Elizabeth. Each time we lowered one of our paddles into the ocean, the water lit up with tiny white fireworks because of the phosphorescence.

In a moment of spontaneous exuberance, Elizabeth exclaimed, "This is the greatest experience of my life!" For both of us, that was a night of wonder as we reveled in the luminous beauty of the star-studded sky above us and the sparkling phosphorescence in the water around us.

Have you ever felt profound wonder in the face of beauty? Perhaps it was in nature, or through music or art, or in the company of a loved one. If you can imagine this moment and feel the wonder of it again, you may get a small glimpse of what God feels when he sees you.

Whenever we experience wonder in the face of beauty, we are catching a little reflection of God's countenance as God beholds *us*. As Simone Weil puts it, "The beauty of the world is the tender smile of Christ to us through matter."[4] God's heart bursts with delight and joy over us—so much so that he spared nothing to pursue us. He came for us that first Christmas as a baby in Jesus, and he absorbed our sin and shame on the cross so we would not have to bear it anymore. As Paul writes in

Romans 5:8, "But God showed his great love for us by sending Christ to die for us while we were still sinners" (NLT).

We Become the Beauty

When we meditate on beauty, we become more beautiful ourselves.

According to Scripture, we begin to look like whatever we worship (see Psalm 115:4–8). If we worship idols—putting money, possessions, or success at the center of our existence—we will become as deaf, dumb, and lifeless as those idols. When we lose our capacity to hear and speak the truth, we insulate ourselves from the Creator God, who is our true source of life. But when we worship the living God, we will find ourselves growing more like him—alive and free.

Neuroscience research confirms that our brains become like the objects we pay attention to. If we meditate on a "god" we perceive as racist, judgmental, and misogynist, we will activate areas in our brain that generate fear and anger, and we will become angrier and more judgmental.[5] As we've noted, "Where attention goes, neural firing flows, and neural connection grows."

Sadly, according to a Baylor University study, nearly 50 percent of Americans believe God is critical and harsh. Only 23 percent view God as loving and benevolent.[6] No wonder Christians are often viewed as angry and judgmental!

But if we meditate on a God who is loving, joyous, and beautiful—and Scripture confirms this as the character of God, which can be seen most clearly in Jesus Christ

(Colossians 1:15)—we will become these things, and we will be both spiritually and neurologically transformed.

Long before we began to understand this dynamic through neuroscience, the apostle Paul intuitively understood this and wrote: "We all, with unveiled face, beholding the glory of the Lord, are being transformed into the same image from one degree of glory to another" (2 Corinthians 3:18 ESV). King David also poetically described this desire to be transformed by gazing on the beauty of the Lord in Psalm 27: "One thing I ask from the LORD, this only do I seek: that I may dwell in the house of the LORD all the days of my life, to gaze on the beauty of the LORD and to seek him in his temple" (v. 4).

Although some of David's choices were selfish and destructive (he committed both adultery and murder), he experienced God's forgiveness and redemption, and his soul became more beautiful as he was restored to his original glory in the presence of God. As David came into the glorious presence of God, fully aware that he was a sinner, he did not feel condemnation, but rather, as he describes in Psalm 34:5:

> Those who look to him are radiant;
>> their faces are never covered with shame.

We Bring the Beauty

Dr. Elaine Scarry, a professor of literature at Harvard, writes, "The beholder of beauty seeks to bring new beauty into the world."[7] This desire to bring new beauty into the world surely inspired Vedran Smajlovic, the lead cellist in the Sarajevo opera, on May 28, 1992, to put on his formal black tails and sit down in a bomb crater and play Albinoni's *Adagio in G minor.* The bomb crater was outside a bakery in his neighborhood, where, on the previous day, twenty-two people had been killed while waiting in the bakery line. For the next twenty-two days—one day for each victim of the bombing, amidst the rubble and the crossfire of snipers and artillery gunners, he decided to challenge the chaotic destruction of war by pointing people toward a better way with his only weapon—beauty.

When we experience beauty ourselves, we want to bring more beauty into the world. This desire may not be a conscious one. Public health data confirms that our contact with the natural world inspires awe and energizes us to share our resources more generously with others. For example, research from the University of California suggests that experiencing awe can prompt us to act in more loving ways toward others. In one study, participants were asked to rate the frequency with which they feel awe and then complete a test that measures generous behavior. The study found that those who experience awe more often tend to behave more generously, even after accounting for other positive emotions, such as compassion or love.

In another experiment on the UC Berkeley campus, one group of participants gazed up at a grove of towering eucalyptus trees for one minute while others, who were standing in the same vicinity, stared at the side of a large building. Then a researcher "accidentally" dropped a box of pens. Participants who had been looking up at the awe-inspiring trees came over and helped pick up more pens than the participants who were staring at the building.[8]

In *A World of Ideas II*, Bill Moyers records the memory of

reporter Jacob Needleman, who observed the launch of Apollo 17 in 1975:

> It was a night launch, and there were hundreds of cynical reporters all over the lawn, drinking beer, wisecracking, and waiting for this 35-story-high rocket.
>
> The countdown came, and then the launch. The first thing you see is this extraordinary orange light, which is just at the limit of what you can bear to look at. Everything is illuminated with this light. Then comes this thing slowly rising up in total silence, because it takes a few seconds for the sound to come across. You hear a "WHOOOOOSH! HHHHMMMM!" It enters right into you.
>
> You can practically hear jaws dropping. The sense of wonder fills everyone in the whole place, as this thing goes up and up. The first stage ignites this beautiful blue flame. It becomes like a star, but you realize there are humans on it. And then there's total silence.
>
> People just get up quietly, helping each other up. They're kind. They open doors. They look at one another, speaking quietly and interestedly. These were suddenly moral people because the sense of wonder, the experience of wonder, had made them moral.[9]

Many of us think the experience of beauty is a luxury, perhaps for the wealthy or those with a lot of time for leisure, but it is essential for the health of our souls, as it frees us from our self-absorption and shame. As the journalists at the Apollo 17 launch discovered, beauty and wonder inspire us to relate to others with more kindness and respect. In our fractured world, where there is so much *othering* of people who are different from us, the experience of beauty is not a luxury, it's a necessity.

But we don't have to watch a rocket launch or stand on the precipice of the Grand Canyon to experience beauty that will transform us.

Abraham Goldberg, a professor at the University of South Carolina, conducted a statistical analysis of happiness in five cities: New York City, Toronto, London, Paris, and Berlin.[10] Goldberg and his research colleagues analyzed earlier Gallup happiness surveys and also collected their own data. They found that what caused people the most happiness in each of these cities was not primarily some of the usual happiness markers people think of such as wealth, career, or status. To the surprise of the researchers, everyday happiness was most easily attained by people as they experienced beauty in their city each day by putting themselves in the path of parks, green spaces, cobblestone streets, history, and lovely architecture. This had a profound effect on their happiness. The study showed that the cumulative positive effects of daily beauty was subtle but strong.

How might you arrange your life so you make it a practice to encounter beauty at least once a day?

Each morning, before checking my smartphone or any electronic device, I run through our neighborhood with our golden retriever, Sasha, then around a nearby park with lovely maple trees before returning home and beginning my workday.

Take a moment to imagine yourself moving through a typical day where you live. How might you arrange your life so you make it a practice to encounter beauty at least once a day?

Perhaps you could enjoy some time each day outdoors,

either in your yard or walking down a favorite street in your neighborhood. Or cultivating a garden. Or enjoying a plant inside your home.

Putting yourself in the pathway of beauty may mean—

Listening to gorgeous music or the waves of the ocean

Pausing before a beautiful building

Enjoying a painting

Taking time to learn to draw or paint

Relishing a good novel, memoir, or film

Making a favorite recipe or a new one

As you intentionally place yourself on the pathway of beauty, may you awaken to the presence of God in the world—Christ's "tender smile" to you through the "matter" of the world. And may you become and bring forth the beauty you long to see in the world.

Prayer Exercise

Close your eyes and take several deep breaths, inhaling and exhaling through your nose.

As you breathe deeply, visualize a particular moment when you experienced a sense of wonder in the face of beauty—perhaps a night when you looked up at the sky and beheld its celestial beauty, or a time when you were transported while listening to music at a concert, or a recent sumptuous meal that you enjoyed, or a moment when you savored the company of a loved one, or something else that moved you. As you feel the wonder of this moment, remember this is a small glimpse of what God feels when he sees you.

Reflection

In all that awakens within us the pure and authentic sentiment of beauty, there is, truly, the presence of God. There is a kind of incarnation of God in the world, of which beauty is the sign.[11]

Study Guide Questions

1. How does beauty free us from self-absorption and leave less room for shame to work?

2. How can beauty awaken us to the love of God?
3. What is the relationship between experiencing beauty and bringing justice to the world?
4. How can you put yourself on the path of beauty?

Chapter 10

CHOOSING JOY

*Joy does not simply happen to us. We have to choose
joy and keep choosing it every day.*
—HENRI NOUWEN

The actor Martin Sheen (also known as Ramón Estévez) starred in the movie *Apocalypse Now*, but he is probably best known for playing the role of President Bartlett in the TV series *The West Wing*. Sheen grew up as one of ten children in a poor Irish-Spanish immigrant family. After his roles in *Apocalypse Now* and *Gandhi*, he experienced a crisis in midlife, and began abusing alcohol. As he struggled with feelings of insecurity and anger, his family nearly broke up.

Then, while Sheen was working in France, his mentor Terrence Malick gave him a copy of Dostoyevsky's *The Brothers Karamazov*, which helped Sheen recognize his longing to be loved and to live an honest and free life in the presence of God. During this period in Paris, he walked to a little Catholic church one day, sat down in a pew, and began to pray. Sheen says that moment of coming back to God was "the single most joyful moment of my life because I knew I had come home to myself . . . This satisfaction has lasted all these years. I'm still on the honeymoon . . . [What] I longed for and, I think, all of us really long for, is knowing that we are loved . . . that despite ourselves, we are loved."[1]

Sheen's experience of being found by God and discovering a kind of love he could never earn became the foundation for life-long joy, which helped him overcome his deep insecurities and propelled him into a life of pursuing justice on behalf of others.

When we realize we are truly loved by God, we experience unfettered joy and ultimately shame cannot survive this joy.

As we've noted, while we can experience multiple emotions at the same time, the feelings of joy and shame are incompatible. When we feel joy, shame gets flushed out, and our spirits can flourish. Because shame resides not just as an idea in our mind but also in our body (through our central nervous system), our experience of healing not only requires the eradication of an idea but also a movement toward emotional and spiritual wholeness that is fostered by the experience of joy. Psychologist Dr. Hillary McBride, in *The Wisdom of Your Body*, writes, "Joy helps us expand, heal, and continue to thrive." In this final chapter, we will explore how joy can help us overcome shame.[2]

Some people think joy is something you catch like the flu—you either have it or you don't, and there's not much you can do about it. But according to Scripture, joy is a choice. Even in adverse circumstances, we can choose to attend to unchanging realities that can make our hearts glad.

However, at the outset of this chapter let me offer one word of caution. If your lows are feeling especially long or deep, you may be experiencing depression, in which case joy will feel elusive. If you find yourself in this place, a physician, counselor, or pastor can help you attend to physiological, psychological, relational, and spiritual factors that may be at play. It is also crucial to walk with supportive, empathetic friends.

The apostle Paul's letter to the church at Philippi pulsates with joy, as he uses the word "joy" or "rejoice" sixteen times. Yet Paul is not writing this letter from an idyllic retreat center overlooking the Mediterranean, but rather from a prison cell in Rome. As Paul waits to stand trial before Caesar, he doesn't know whether he is going to live or die, but he is *not* a nervous wreck because he is *choosing* to rejoice.

Gratitude as a Pathway to Joy

Shawn Achor, a Harvard-trained psychologist, says, "If I know everything about your external world, I can only predict 10% of your long-term happiness. 90% of your long-term happiness is predicted not by the external world, but by the way your brain processes the world."[3]

Paul was able to experience joy even in prison because he had trained his mind and spirit to process his external world through the lens of celebration. Raised as a devout Jew, Paul would have gone to every Jewish festival over the course of his life. Year after year, he would have participated in the Feast of Tabernacles, when the Jews live for a brief time in makeshift tents to remind themselves that God delivered their ancestors out of slavery in Egypt and led them through the desert to the promised land. This feast also reminds Jews that, in time, God will put all things right in the world. By celebrating what God did in the past along with what God will do in the future, Jews regularly practice rhythms that usher them into the experience of joy.

Scholars estimate that perhaps a third of the days in the Hebrew calendar in Paul's first-century world were made up of these feast days, so they had plenty of regular times throughout the year to joyfully celebrate what God had done and what God was going to do in the future while gathering together to enjoy sweet drinks and delicious food!

While in prison, Paul made it a regular practice to rejoice in the Lord and to pray with thanksgiving (Philippians 4:4–7). When we remind ourselves of what God has done in the past and live with an awareness that God holds the future and will one day redeem all things, then we can experience an undercurrent of joy—even during our most painful moments and seasons.

Though we may not be celebrating a feast day every three days, we can establish regular rhythms of giving thanks.

Each evening over dinner, our little family offers thanks for what we are most grateful for in the day. For our adolescent son, Joey, it may be good weather (it rains a lot in Vancouver, so we celebrate whenever the sun makes an appearance), or it may be the good dinner we are enjoying in that moment. For my wife, Sakiko, it might be making progress with a translation project she's working on or a meaningful conversation she's had with someone. For me, it could be a good run through a forest trail with Sasha, our golden retriever, or hearing about a breakthrough in someone's life. This simple exercise helps train our mind and spirit to look for God's gifts in our world.

Our amygdala, the alarm center of our brain, uses about

two-thirds of its neurons to look for bad news. Scientists believe that our ancient ancestors developed this negative bias to survive as they scanned the horizon on the African savannah, looking out for predators who might want to enjoy them for lunch. But establishing a regular thanksgiving exercise helps rebalance our brain toward the positive and orients us to look for God actively working in our midst.[4]

In mid-March of 2020, our family had planned to use saved points to enjoy a trip to our favorite vacation spot in Hawaii. But at the last minute, we decided to stay home because of the COVID-19 outbreak. Naturally, we were disappointed.

As I reflected on this canceled trip, I remembered how, on a previous trip to Hawaii, I had walked on the beach under the stars on our first night, thanking God for various things he had done throughout my lifetime, and my heart had exploded with gratitude and joy. That night ended up being the high point of my week of vacation.

A few weeks after we had to cancel our trip to Hawaii, I was walking around a park not far from our home, giving thanks to God for things he had done in my life, and once again my heart exploded with gratitude and joy. I realized I was feeling just as happy as I had on that magical beach walk on my first night in Hawaii. I thought, *I don't really need to go to an exotic tropical island, because I can experience joy right here in my hometown.*

On the first day of any vacation, and fairly regularly on my Sabbath day, I do a lifelong prayer of Examen, where I give thanks to God for the gifts across my lifetime. I often take a long, slow walk, ideally on the beach or in the woods. As I begin, I pray that the Holy Spirit would guide the time, and then I start to recount the events of my life, beginning with my birth in Tokyo. I thank God for the love and welcome of my parents and my grandmother around the time of my birth. Though I obviously don't remember any of this, I know it shaped who I am.

Then I thank God for leading our family across the ocean and a continent to New York City. Again, I don't remember our brief time there, but I thank God for the small third birthday party I've been told I had there. Then I give thanks to God for our family's move to London, England, where I have my first memories. As a three-year-old, our family lived in a small townhome on Red Post Hill. I remember receiving some second-hand clothes that looked pretty much new from a family with a son who was slightly older than me, and I thank God for this provision.

Next, I thank God for our move from England to Vancouver, Canada—by ship through the Panama Canal—when I was seven.

As I trace my life forward, I thank God for the crisis in adolescence that opened my heart to Christ. I thank God for the doors he opened for me to go to school, the provision of places to live, the sense of calling to my life work, all my friends, my life partner, Sakiko, and my son, Joey. I even thank God for the painful moments in my life that he has, in time, redeemed. By the end of this Prayer of Examen, as David writes in Psalm 139, I have a profound sense that God has hemmed me in, behind and before, that he has laid his hand upon me. And with David, I feel this "knowledge is too wonderful for me, too lofty for me to attain" (Psalm 139:6).

This exercise of gratitude awakens and prolongs a sense of joy in my life.

As noted in chapter 6 ("Overcoming Envy"), about 50 percent of our happiness is based on a "set point." External circumstances account for only 10 percent, but a whopping 40 percent of our happiness is determined by *intentional* activity. One intentional activity that can powerfully boost our happiness and sense of well-being is a regular practice of gratitude.

Robert Emmons, a professor of psychology who is widely considered the world's leading expert on gratitude, points out that practicing gratitude can reshape our brain and actually raise our set point of happiness.[5] When we experience joyful gratitude, we live out of a sense that we have enough *and* that we are enough.[6]

Joy comes from framing our past in light of the good things God has already done—and trusting for the good things God will continue to do in the future.

Expecting something painful can be discouraging. In the spring of 2020, at the beginning of the COVID-19 pandemic, many of us were experiencing anguish, because we were anticipating a future of unknown grief.

Conversely, anticipating something good coming into our life brings us joy.

In the movie *Shadowlands*, which is based on the life of C. S. Lewis, Lewis (played by Anthony Hopkins) says, "The most joy lies not in the having but in the desiring."[7] When we are in the midst of hardship, anticipating something good on the horizon can fill us with consolation and hope.

Recently, Sakiko, Joey, and I watched *The Lord of the Rings* trilogy. As those of you familiar with the story already know, it is an epic, full of darkness and danger, where the hobbit, Frodo, is summoned to take the One Ring and destroy it in the fires of Mount Doom.

But this was Joey's first time seeing these movies, and he didn't know how things would end. While he was captivated by this great tale, he also experienced anxiety, because he didn't know how the story would conclude. I think he felt a little like Frodo's friend Sam Gamgee, who asks, "How could the end be happy when so much bad had happened?"

But Sakiko and I had already seen the movies. Though we had forgotten many of the details, we knew there would be a happy ending, and so we enjoyed the story with less anxiety and more anticipatory joy.

When we trust that God will one day bring good out of every evil in our lives and make the world right, we can live with a greater sense of peace and joy. Though we may be going through darkness and danger or living through a harrowing chapter, because we know that God is guiding our story, we can trust that we will eventually discover that we are living through a *good* book. The tale of our life will ultimately prove to be a comedy, in the literary sense, rather than a tragedy because our final end will be joyous.

In Fyodor Dostoyevsky's great novel *The Brothers Karamazov*, Ivan Karamazov says:

> I believe like a child that suffering will be healed and made up for, that all the humiliating absurdity of human contradictions will vanish like a pitiful mirage . . . that in the world's finale, at the moment of eternal harmony, something so precious will come to pass that it will suffice for all hearts, for the comforting of all resentments, for the

atonement of all the crimes of humanity, for all the blood that they've shed; that it will make it not only possible to forgive but to justify all that has happened.[8]

The path of joy leads us to look back and give thanks to God—and also to look ahead with faith, trusting that God holds the future in his hands.

Live Well

Another way to cultivate joy is to embrace activities that help us feel more alive.

An American Psychological Association study found that we tend to overestimate how certain activities will lift us up, especially when we are under stress. Activities such as gambling, drinking, shopping, playing video games, surfing the internet, or watching TV or movies for more than two hours may seem appealing and will momentarily make us feel better because they release dopamine in our brain, but in the end they bring us down, often making us feel a little more depressed than we were before.

Conversely, the same study found that we tend to underestimate the power of other activities to bring us a sense of well-being. These include playing sports, playing or listening to music, spending time with friends and family, praying or attending a worship service, going outside for a walk, getting a massage, meditating, yoga, or engaging in a hobby.[9] Rather than releasing a brief shot of dopamine to our brain, these activities boost the mood-enhancing chemicals serotonin and oxytocin, which tend to bring us a longer-lasting sense of well-being.

These psychological findings correlate with the spiritual experiences of Ignatius of Loyola in the sixteenth century. At the age of twenty-six, Ignatius had an opportunity to achieve the kind of military glory he had fantasized about since he was a young boy. But at the battle for Pamplona, he was severely wounded by a cannonball that injured both of his legs. While recovering, Ignatius found himself daydreaming about becoming a famous knight. He also longed to read romance novels and fantasized about winning the love of a great lady.[10] But instead, he was given books on the life of Jesus and the lives of saints, which inspired Ignatius with a love for God and spiritual things. During this period, Ignatius observed how his old ambitions of becoming a famous knight and daydreams of winning the hand of a lady left him "dry and sad," but his new desires for following Jesus and growing in holiness gave him lasting joy and consolation.

This crucial discovery went on to inform Ignatius's classic work *Spiritual Exercises*, which instructs those seeking to discern God's will to consider not just the beginning of an experience, but also the middle and the end of the experience. There are times when something that initially seems to lift us up ends up bringing us down. When we can see the "tail of the serpent" emerging in the middle and end of an experience, this is a sign that we are not acting in line with God's will for our lives. Being in God's will is typically accompanied by a joy that *lasts*. Similarly, St. Anthony observed that you can only tell whether you have been visited by a devil or an angel by how you feel afterward. What kind of activities bring you a sense of unfettered and prolonged joy and draw you to God?

Some of us experience deep joy as we do something physical outdoors, such as running on a forest trail, hiking up a mountain, or kayaking on the ocean.

Others abandon themselves to joy while listening to a piece of stirring music or standing in front of a beautiful work of art.

Some are transported into joy when they get lost in a captivating novel or movie.

Others experience great delight as they savor coffee or relish delicious food.

And many feel a sense of deep and abiding joy when they spend time with someone they love.

Any practice that makes us come alive over time, even if it is not overtly religious, is a *spiritual* practice. Whenever we experience the pleasure of play, we are given a window into God's abounding pleasure in us. If you feel joyful pleasure is a frivolous and unnecessary luxury, remember that joy is God's invention and intention for us. God calls us to a life of joy. According to Scripture, we will be held to account for our *failure* to enjoy the life we have been given.[11]

> *Any practice that makes us come alive over time, even if it is not overtly religious, is a* spiritual *practice.*

In C. S. Lewis's *The Screwtape Letters*, a senior devil coaches a junior demon by offering the following observation about the "Enemy" (who, in this context, is God):

> [God is] a hedonist at heart. All those fasts and vigils and stakes and crosses are only a facade. Or only like foam on the seashore. Out at sea, out in His sea, there is pleasure, and more pleasure. He makes no secret of it; at His right hand are "pleasures for evermore. . . ."

He has filled His world full of pleasures. There are things for humans to do all day long without His minding in the least—sleeping, washing, eating, drinking, making love, playing, praying, working. Everything has to be *twisted* before it's any use to us. We fight under the cruel disadvantages. Nothing is naturally on our side.[12]

The senior devil concedes that God is the author of joy, and thus pleasure must be *twisted* for it to be of any use to evil.

As Lewis observes, God is the author of pleasure, and so God delights in our delight.

Honor Sabbath Rhythms

One way to cultivate our sense of God's delight is through the practice of Sabbath. The book of Isaiah describes this sacred day as a source of delight (Isaiah 58:13–14). Mark Buchanan says Sabbath is a day where "we cease from what is necessary and embrace what gives life."[13] The Jewish theologian Abraham Joshua Heschel describes Sabbath as a "palace in time."[14] In the best way, the Sabbath command can compel us to stop so we can enjoy God, life, and the most important people in our lives.

Because I tend to be a workaholic, if Sabbath were merely a suggestion from God, I would likely pass on it. But because it's one of the Ten Commandments, and I don't want to break any of them by choice, it forces me, in a good way, to stop and to enjoy God, the many gifts in my daily life, and my most important relationships. Without the Sabbath commandment, my marriage would be compromised, and my relationships with my family and close friends would be hurt.

Sabbath does not need to be an isolated time where we withdraw from human contact. Instead, Sabbath can be a gift from God when we are free to invest our lives in others. Even if you're not a workaholic, Sabbath frees you to delight in life and the people who are most important to you—whether this means connecting with family or friends in person or using Facetime, Zoom, or a phone if they live far away—without feeling guilty about not working productively.

According to psychologist Shawn Achor, there is one thing—and only one thing—that unites the happiest 10 percent of people in the world. It's not living in a warm climate, nor their level of education, their income, their race, their cultural background, or even their physical health. Rather, the single thing that unites the top 10 percent of the happiest people in the world is the quality of their relationships. One of the best predictors of experiencing joy in a day is whether you did or did not have meaningful contact with friends or relatives. Daniel Kahneman, the Nobel Prize-winning economist, writes: "It is only a slight exaggeration to say that happiness is the experience of spending time with people you love and who love you."[15]

> *The single thing that unites the top 10 percent of the happiest people in the world is the quality of their relationships.*

We can know deep pleasure when we regularly experience the gift of Sabbath rest and use this gift to connect in meaningful ways with those we love.

Discovering Joy
through Service

As we've seen in this book, one of the paradoxes of life is that by giving away our lives as we serve others, we find joy.

Anthony Ray Hinton spent thirty years (1985–2015) on death row for a crime he did not commit. When the crime he was accused of committing took place, he was working in a locked factory fifteen miles away. But when he was arrested in the state of Alabama, he was told by the police officers that he would be going to jail simply because he was *black*.

When he was sent to death row after a trial that was a complete travesty of justice, he was angry and heartbroken. He ended up spending thirty years in solitary confinement in a five-foot by seven-foot cell, from which he was allowed out only one hour a day. In reflecting on this time in prison, he says, "When no one believes a word you say, eventually you stop saying anything. I did not say, 'Good Morning.' I did not say, 'Good Evening.' I did not say, 'How are you?' to anyone." He continues:

> If the guards needed some information from me, I wrote it down on a piece of paper. I was angry. Then, going into my fourth year, I heard a man in a cell next to mine crying. The love and compassion I had received from my mother spoke through me and I asked him what was wrong. He said he just found out that his mother had passed away. I told him, "Look at it this way. Now you have someone in heaven who's going to argue your case

160

before God." And then I told him a joke and he laughed. Suddenly my voice and my sense of humor were back. And for 26 long years after that night, I tried to focus on other people's problems. I asked myself, "How can I live in service for others," and every day I did, I would get to the end of the day and realize I had not focused on my own problems.[16]

As Hinton focused on serving others in prison, instead of growing into a person of anger and bitterness, he grew into a person of joy.

Hinton, who is a committed Christian and was eventually retried, found innocent, and released from prison, demonstrates, along with the apostle Paul, that regardless of our circumstances—even if we are in prison unjustly—with God's help, we can choose the path of joy. When we grow in love, we will experience joy as we realize we are becoming more and more like our Creator God.

In Philippians 1, Paul writes from a prison cell, "I always pray [for you] with joy . . . being confident of this, that he who began a good work in you will carry it on to completion until the day of Christ Jesus" (Philippians 1:4, 6). If we want to feel good for a moment, we can choose cocaine, pornography, promiscuous sex, impulse shopping, gambling, or something else that will give us an instant dopamine hit. But these momentary highs will eventually leave us feeling worse. There is a big difference between self-medicating and Spirit-led self-care. If we want to know real, long-lasting joy, we need to allow God to form us into the masterpiece he imagined when he first created us.

Joyfully Fulfilling Our Purpose

The ancient Greek philosophers did not believe that the purpose of life was to be happy in the sense of being in a good mood all the time. Rather, they proposed that the purpose of life was to experience *eudaimonia*, which can be translated as "fulfillment" and can be understood as being very close to joy, akin to a sense of "joyful fulfillment." What distinguishes happiness from *eudaimonia*, or joyful fulfillment, is pain. It is possible to suffer physically or psychologically and yet experience joyful fulfillment. Certain kinds of work can be very demanding, such as raising children, maintaining a relationship, or developing a particular profession or craft, but we can also experience fulfillment and meaning by taking up these demanding tasks in love and letting the challenges transform us and awaken us into joy.[17]

We can face hardships, perhaps even heartbreak, and still experience joyful fulfillment as the Holy Spirit reveals to us that we are making a difference in the lives of others and that God is causing all things ultimately to work together for good so we can share in the likeness of Jesus (Romans 8:28–29).

G. K. Chesterton poetically wondered, "If seeds in the black earth can turn into such beautiful roses, what might not the heart of man [or woman] become in its long journey toward the stars?"[18] Similarly, the psychiatrist Elizabeth Kübler-Ross observes, "The most beautiful people we have known are those who have known defeat, known suffering, known struggle, known loss, and have found their way out of the depths. These persons have an appreciation, a sensitivity, and an understanding of life that fills them with compassion, gentleness, and a deep loving concern. Beautiful people do not just happen."[19]

As I write these words, my mother's cancer has returned. While she has never smoked, she was diagnosed with lung cancer a few years ago. Though she had a successful operation, the cancer has now spread to her spine and pancreas. She has decided not to pursue further treatment but is at peace.

My mother lives with my brother's family, which is about a twelve-minute walk from our home in Vancouver. My three sisters have flown in from Montréal, San Francisco, and Southern California to be with her.

> *"Beautiful people do not just happen."*
> —Elizabeth Kübler-Ross

It is hard to see her in physical pain, especially when she is retching. There are times these days when she would like her life on earth to be over, to be liberated from her suffering and fully alive in the presence of Jesus. But mostly, she is full of peace. Although she has lost more than thirty pounds and now weighs about a mere seventy pounds, and though the bones in her arms are visible under her sagging skin, I have never seen her more luminously joyful. Everyone who has come into contact with her recently—her children, the palliative care nurse, and even the young man who dropped off an adjustable hospital bed for her—can see that she is brilliantly and beautifully incandescent.

I have had a front-row seat to my mother's life for more than half a century now and have heard stories from each chapter of her life. As a young girl in war-torn Japan, she lived with her grandmother in the countryside during a time when children were evacuated from the cities to rural communities to minimize their exposure to bombs. Her mother would occasionally send her chocolates or cookies, but her grandmother would snatch them, toss them in the air, and catch them in her mouth, just to torment my mother. Sometimes my mom was so hungry that she ate flowers in a nearby field.

After the war, she asked her father, who had run successful businesses to support the war effort, to allow her to study in America. In this more traditional era, he said, "If you study in America, no man will ever marry you!" She responded, "I'll swim across the ocean!" He relented and supported her studies at leading universities in America.

Not long after she returned to Japan, much to her father's surprise, she got engaged to the man who would eventually become my dad. Her father, then at the height of his career as an entrepreneur, chartered a plane to bring guests from Tokyo to the southern city of Kagoshima for the wedding ceremony.

After she and my dad were married and our family had moved to Vancouver, my dad worked for a few years as a writer for a newsletter on the Canadian economy for Japanese corporations. It had a small circulation, and our family struggled financially. When I was nine years old, I remember receiving donated toys at Christmas and food hampers from our local church.

Throughout my mom's years of privilege, she did not grow smug and conceited. And during her experience of financial deprivation, though it was frustrating and anxiety provoking at times, she did not grow embittered.

My waywardness as a teenager caused her to recommit her life to Christ, and I have had the gift of seeing her steady transformation over the years as she has grown more and more into the likeness of Christ. She has gone from being overly focused on her children's educational advancement to expressing that character and kindness are more important than intelligence or academic achievement. She has also gone from being somewhat prone to anxiety to exhibiting a growing peace and mellowness of soul as she entrusts her life more fully to God.

A couple of weeks ago, at a small gathering around her bed, some family members offered words to honor her. Our adolescent son, among other things, thanked his grandmother for her kindness by blurting out his appreciation for her generous gift of cash on his birthday and chocolate cupcakes. My mother beamed and retorted, "I have so much respect for you, Joey. You're so genuine, authentic, you never put on pretenses. I want to become more like you."

Although she didn't use these precise words, even as she was on the brink of eternity she wanted to shed some of her last vestiges of needing to look good in front of others, in order to become her true self.

If, as you experience the high points and valleys of your life, you also discover that God is weaving together the details of your life, you will experience the wonder of gratitude. As you experience the pleasure of doing things that make you come alive and the delight of serving others, you will become the beautiful masterpiece God created you to be, and you will radiate the light of your original glory—your truest and most incandescent self—into the world.

Prayer Exercise

Take several deep breaths, slowly inhaling and exhaling through your nose. As you continue to breathe deeply, close your eyes and invite the Spirit to guide you through the high points and valleys of your life journey to this point.

As you remember each significant transition or moment in your life, take a deep breath, inhaling, *Thank you for this part of my journey.* Then exhale, *I trust you to write a good story with my life.*

Before opening your eyes, invite the Spirit to awaken all of your senses in the coming week—your eyes, ears, mouth, nose, body, mind, heart—to engage in practices that will lead you on the path to a more abundant life and a prolonged experience of unfettered pleasure and deepening joy.

Reflection

As you trust God to weave together all the details and experiences of your life, you will begin to live joyfully into the *good* ending already imagined for your story.

Study Guide Questions

1. How does joy help us overcome shame? How can you choose joy each day? How can you practice gratitude each day?

2. Recall a time when you experienced the joy of anticipating something good in your future. How can you nurture the belief that God holds your future?

3. What are some activities that bring you joy and draw you to God? How might you engage these activities as a pathway of delight?

4. How might a regular Sabbath practice lead you on a pathway of joy?

NOTHING WASTED

Christ has no body now on earth but yours.
—SAINT TERESA OF ÁVILA,
SIXTEENTH-CENTURY MYSTIC

As a pastor, from time to time, I will hear a person's confession. Across the years, people have confessed all kinds of sins, including theft, adultery, slander, and even taking someone's life—virtually every one of the Ten Commandments, and other transgressions as well.

A person will typically experience a certain level of guilt and shame because of what they have done, but their shame will be magnified if someone important to them becomes aware of their failure or if it's widely exposed through gossip, social media, or the news. We all know that it's one thing to fail, but it's much worse if our failure is exposed to other people.

By these standards, Jesus's disciple Peter would have experienced shame on the grandest scale, as his abysmal failure took place in the actual presence of Jesus. What's more, it went on to become widely known—not only by his peers and family but also to a vast number of people—as it was recorded in the pages of the Bible, which is by far the most widely read book of all time. The following is a recollection of that infamous failure.

On the Mount of Olives, on the night before Jesus was crucified on the cross, he indicated that all his disciples would desert him. Peter spoke up and boasted, "Even if everyone else loses courage and caves in, I will stand with you!"

But Jesus replied, "Before the rooster crows, you will have denied me three times."

Peter pushed back, "Even if it means I die, I will never deny you!"

Soon after this exchange, Jesus was arrested by armed guards at the base of the Mount of Olives in the garden of Gethsemane. Peter then followed Jesus at a distance. As he stood in a courtyard by a charcoal fire, trying to keep warm, a servant girl recognized him and said, "He was with Jesus."

"No, I was not," Peter replied.

Then others who were gathered around the fire said to him, "Aren't you one of his disciples?"

"No," he insisted again.

Then a relative of the man whose ear Peter had cut off said, "Didn't I see you in the garden with him? Surely, you're with Jesus." But Peter denied it again and started cursing.

Immediately a rooster crowed. On the other side of the courtyard gate, Jesus turned and looked straight at Peter.

Peter's face fell with shame. He could not look at Jesus. When Jesus had needed him most, Peter had disowned him—betrayed him.

In this ancient Near Eastern culture, where people relied more heavily on nonverbal communication, Peter's face dropping and his body curling in on itself would have revealed his shame to those gathered around the fire. He would have also felt terribly demeaned in his own eyes.

And so, he wept bitterly.

After Jesus was crucified, Peter and some of the other disciples decided to return to their former work of fishing. One evening, they went out and fished through the night, but caught nothing.

At dawn, the resurrected Jesus was standing on the shore, but the disciples didn't recognize him. Jesus shouted to them, "Throw your net over the right side of the boat." They did, and caught so many fish they couldn't even pull in the net!

Immediately recognizing the man on the shore as Jesus, Peter dove into the lake and swam toward him! When Peter got to shore, he approached Jesus, who was roasting fish and bread over a charcoal fire. The sight and smell of a charcoal fire would have filled Peter's chest with a sense of shame, reminding him of his colossal failure around the charcoal fire the night he denied Jesus.

"Come, let's have some breakfast," Jesus said.

After they had breakfast, Jesus said to Peter, "Simon, son of John, do you love me?"

Peter answered, "Yes, Lord! You know that I love you!"

"Feed my lambs," Jesus said.

Jesus repeated his question a second time, "Simon, son of John, do you love me?"

Peter answered, "Yes, my Lord! You know that I love you!"

"Take care of my sheep," Jesus said.

Then Jesus asked him again, "Peter, son of John, do you love me?"

Peter was saddened by being asked this question a third

time, and so he said, "Lord, you know everything. You know that I love you!"

Jesus replied, "Feed my lambs."

Jesus didn't give Peter three opportunities to express his love because Jesus was feeling insecure and wanted to be reassured of Peter's love. Rather, in the wake of Peter's three denials, Jesus wanted to offer *him* a path of true and complete healing and restoration.

Jesus had brought Peter to a charcoal fire, the sight, sound, and smell of which would have evoked his past failure, so he could experience healing. Modern counseling methods and healing prayer practices confirm the wisdom of Jesus's gentle and loving process in this story, as both have found that re-engaging a painful memory *and* adding an element so the person feels safe, soothed, and secure can help diminish the pain and trauma of that memory and lead to deeper healing.[1]

Revisiting Our Pain and Shame

A few years ago, I was leading a group of people through a time of silent centering prayer on Vancouver Island. I didn't know it at the time, but one of the participants had accidentally backed his minivan over his two-year-old daughter several months earlier. At first, he recoiled when I said I would create space for silent prayer, because every time he had entered into silence since the accident, the memory would resurface in a painful way.

But during this time of silent meditative prayer, Jesus came to this man carrying his two-year-old daughter in his own arms and then placed her in her father's arms. The man later shared that as he held his daughter, he could feel her weight, and he could also smell her familiar scent. It was a profoundly healing moment for him. Though he misses his daughter terribly and continues to experience real pain over the loss, his experience of sensing both Jesus's and his daughter's physical presence *with him* has brought him ongoing comfort and solace.

When we know Jesus is *with us* in a moment of great pain or shame, we can journey through our grief and humiliation toward healing and wholeness.

When Jesus invites Peter to affirm his love three times, Jesus gently helps Peter revisit his failure to assure him that, despite his denial, Jesus is with him and hasn't given up on him. Each time Peter reaffirms his love, Jesus recommissions him to his life work: "take care of my lambs," "take care of my sheep," "feed my sheep." Regardless of our failures or past, when we come face-to-face with Jesus in confession, we will experience love without condition, and we will be reaffirmed in his calling for us.

Receiving a Life Calling through Our Pain and Shame

When I was a seminary student in Boston, I had breakfast from time to time with an older mentor, who was the pastor of a large church in the area. One morning over scrambled eggs and toast, I said, "You are very gifted and successful and seem so confident. Do you have any fears?"

I knew that while he had been the president of an international student ministry, it had come out that he had committed adultery and had been forced to resign. I also knew he had gone through a process of restoration and, in time, had re-entered pastoral ministry. But this was not on my mind as I asked the question.

My friend looked me straight in the eyes and said, "You're looking at a guy who lost everything, and it was entirely my fault. I realized as I looked through the help wanted section of the *Wall Street Journal*, there's nothing I am qualified to do here. When God gave me back my life's work, I was overcome with a sense of awe and gratitude. My greatest fear is that I would lose this sense of wonder."

When we encounter the beauty of God's love and forgiveness and receive a commissioning or a recommissioning to our life calling, we experience joyful wonder.

As was true for Peter and my mentor friend, so it can be for us. When we receive Jesus's love, grace, and healing, our failures and shame can become fodder for our growth and lead us into our most important life work. God can and will redeem and use everything in our lives for good. In fact, our failures can be used as compost to nourish the soil of our lives so we will become deeply rooted in the love of God and will, in time, be able to bear great and abundant fruit. From our places of deepest shame, grace flows most freely.

> *When we receive Jesus's love, grace, and healing, our failures and shame can become fodder for our growth and lead us into our most important life work.*

When I first returned to Vancouver as a young pastor, I felt unsure about my suitability to serve in vocational church ministry, so I met with Dr. James Houston, a professor of spiritual theology at Regent College, a nearby seminary. We met in the living room of his home, and, among other things, I mentioned my failure in crossing a boundary with a woman in a public setting when I was a student (which I describe in chapter 4, "Seeing God's Face in Others").

Dr. Houston paused and said, "Well, that may be prophetic."

"What do you mean?" I asked.

I will never forget his reply: "It may be that God is calling you to lead a church where people who have failed in some way are welcomed, loved, and served."

Right in the midst of our greatest failures and deepest shame, God meets us, calls us by name, and gently commissions us to our most powerful life work.

Becoming the Countenance of Christ to the World

Christ is no longer physically with us, as he was for Peter and the original disciples, but he is very much present to us through his church, which the Bible describes as "the body of Christ" (1 Corinthians 12:27). As Teresa of Ávila famously said, "Christ has no body now but yours . . . No hands, no feet on earth but yours. Yours are the eyes through which he looks with compassion on this world. Yours are the feet with which he walks to do good. Yours are the hands through which he blesses all the world . . . Christ has no body now on earth but yours."

If we become the presence of Jesus to one another, instead of being diminished and derailed by our sins, shortcomings, and shame, we will move toward restoration and wholeness, and also be empowered for our life work.

175

While the institutional church at times has rightly been seen as self-righteous, judgmental, and exclusive, gentle healing and loving transformation can occur when we become "the eyes through which he looks with compassion on this world." When we reflect the face of Christ to each other, we help one another become more whole. In our divided, polarized world, as members of the body of Christ—the church—we need to create space in our hearts to welcome one another's most painful and shameful stories.

As a pastor colleague of mine reflected, "When we are feeling suffering and pain, we can choose to perceive God's compassionate gaze falling upon us, and we realize that he feels our pain, we are not alone. In that moment, we also realize that his compassionate gaze is falling on others. He feels their pain and is with them too."

My psychiatrist friend Curt Thompson, who is an elder at his church, told me about "confessional communities," which are small groups of six to eight people who create a safe and secure space together so they can express their grief, trauma, shame, and deep desires in order to tell a "truer story."

In *Soul of Desire*, Curt recounts one confessional community gathering he hosted:

> "I'm having a really hard time saying this," said Brendan, who had been participating in the community for more than a year. He fumbled with his hands and paused, trying to find the courage and the words.
>
> Sarah, another member of the group, said softly, "Take your time. We aren't going anywhere."

"I am actually a little worried that you will go somewhere when you hear what I have to tell you," he said as he began, slowly, unsure of his words.

"Eight years ago, I fathered a child, a daughter. I was making business trips to Europe pretty frequently, and I had an affair that lasted about six months. I eventually told my wife, and we began a painful process of reconciliation that led to healing. But about a year after I broke off the affair, and after my wife and I had started marriage therapy, I got an email from the woman . . . and she told me she had become pregnant with my child and had the baby. She didn't want to reconnect with me, nor did she want the child to have anything to do with me. My wife and I discussed it at length and agreed that I should follow up on it, but the woman never returned any of my emails. I had met the woman in one country, but she lives in another, and I have no idea where either she or the child is. It's like this blight that I carry around that always reminds me of a choice I made that I regret and that I just can't seem to escape."

Curt describes how the group sat in silence for some time, holding the moment.

Then Sarah, who had encouraged Brendan to take his time, finally broke the silence. Her husband had also had an affair, which had led to a divorce when her husband refused to pursue reconciliation and left her and their three children to start a new life on the West Coast. Tearfully, Sarah spoke of her gratitude for Brendan's transparency and acknowledged his genuine remorse. Then she named the palpable shame he was displaying in the presence of these group members and stated she did not want him to remain there. But she also confessed that his words evoked in her sharp feelings of betrayal, anger, shame, and despair as images from the story of her own husband's unfaithfulness began to rush into her consciousness. Nonetheless, she wanted him to be free of his shame, so she expressed that what she most wanted him to hear from her was love in the face of both his pain and her own.

As the rest of the group connected Brendan's story and Sarah's response to their own stories, they expressed their own feelings, which ranged from sorrow to gratitude to anger.

First, Tom expressed gratitude to Brendan for sharing such a vulnerable part of his story, but then he went on to describe the fury he felt as he listened to this news. Though he had not been a paragon of virtue in his own life, he still wanted to trust that there were other men who could model what it meant to live with integrity in the world. He had thought Brendan was one of these men, and now Tom felt the ground shifting under his feet.

Curt reminded the group that evil could co-opt this moment, so he invited them to breathe deeply and attend to the presence of God as they listened to each other.

Next, Gwen, who had been sobbing throughout Brendan's confession, said, "I've never heard a man apologize for much of anything, let alone for this. I want you to know that what you just said has been healing for me."

In telling their own stories, each member of the group expressed love to one another. As they shared vulnerably, they each also took the risk of revealing parts of themselves—without any guarantee that they would be received. But as they stayed with one another, listening authentically and sharing honestly, they reflected the loving face and compassionate voice of Jesus to each other, and they all experienced a beautiful sense of solace and were liberated from shame.[2]

Are there people who have received and can offer the grace of God in your world and with whom you can move toward a place of greater wholeness?

On the occasion of my mentor Leighton Ford's ninetieth birthday, his granddaughter Christine shared that she had once confided in her grandfather about a deep work God had done in her life in the wake of a painful breakup with her boyfriend. After listening to her story, her grandfather wept. With tears streaming down his face, he told her, "I don't think I've known the true Christine until now." Reflecting on this moment, she told those who had gathered to celebrate his long and faithful life, "When you're in his presence there's no judgment, no shame, so you can become your true self."

Her words rang true for me as well. When I am in Leighton's presence, there is no judgment or shame, so I can become my true self. In this way, he has become the *presence* of Christ to me—and to many others.

Rather than judging one another, we can offer God's love and grace to each other as brothers and sisters in the same family of God. When we live, move, and become who we were created to be as the body of Christ, we can live as the countenance of Christ to the world—and our faces will be radiant, without any shadow of shame, and we will boldly declare, "Now I become myself."

Study Guide Questions

1. When Jesus engages Peter's painful memory of failure, how does he create a path of restoration and healing for Peter?

2. How does knowing that Jesus is *with us* in our pain and shame bring us solace and wholeness?

3. How have failure and shame become fodder for growth in your life? How have some of your failures shaped your life work?

4. How can we seek to live as Christ's body in the world to help heal shame and encourage one another to become our true selves?

ACKNOWLEDGMENTS

In chapter 4, I wrote about how we can encounter God's love through others. This book would never have come to life if it wasn't for the loving, skillful, and generous contributions of others.

After I had completed an initial draft of the book, while clearing space on a laptop I accidentally deleted the entire manuscript—both on my computer and in the "cloud" as well. Thanks to the work of Edlyn Hiebert, my can-do, persevering assistant and to my tech-savvy, generous colleague Amrit Carrasco, they were able to recover the about-to-be-permanently deleted files. The files I feared forever gone were brought back to life!

Thank you, Karen Hollenbeck, for offering your exquisite gifts with the English language to help me better express my work.

I am grateful to Craig Pagens, Nick Valadez, Peter Mitham, and Aisling Zweigle for responding to chapters and for your encouragement to write this book—and continue writing.

I am also thankful for Hillary McBride, Curt Thompson, Gregg Ten Elshof, Scott Neufeld, Mark Buchanan, Morris Dirks, John Michael Cusick, N. T. Wright, Ashton Eaton, Simon Sheh,

D. J. Chuang, Elizabeth Archer Klein, Yoji Nakamura, and Leighton Ford for interacting with me and offering insights that helped inform and inspire the writing.

Thank you, Abraham Wu and Victor Chua, for your research.

I am continuously grateful to my colleagues Jade Holownia, Dan Matheson, Craig Pagens, Anthony and Michele Yackel, Laura Wiens, Penny Crosby, and Ryan Lui for their "feedforward" on my (and our) sermons, which helps to feed my preaching and writing and vice versa.

Thank you, Stephanie Martin, for your beautiful cover design!

It is such a gift to work with a remarkable, dedicated, and creative team at Zondervan: Ryan Pazdur, thank you for your empowering belief in and steadfast support for this project; Alexis De Weese, for your contagious enthusiasm; Chris Beetham, for your keen attention to detail.

I am thankful to my late father and mother, who passed during the writing of this book, for their consistent love in which shame ultimately cannot survive.

Thank you, Edlyn Hiebert, for marshaling resources, formatting, and checking and rechecking drafts. Thank you, Shirley Sakowski and Nicholas Steinwand, for meticulous proofreading.

Thank you, Joey, as grandma says, for being so real and authentic!

Sakiko, for being the best conversation partner on the mundane to the sublime and the love of my life.

Thank you to God for wasting nothing and redeeming everything, for making us radiant and free of shame.

NOTES

Chapter 1: The Fear of Not Being Enough

1. Michelle Obama, *Becoming*, narrated by Michelle Obama (New York: Random House Audio, 2018), audiobook, 19 hrs., 3 min.

2. John L. Bishop, *God Distorted: How Your Earthly Father Affects Your Perception of God and Why It Matters* (Colorado Springs: Multnomah, 2013), 87–88.

3. Unresolved guilt and shame release corticoid toxins in our body, which make us more susceptible to all kinds of illness and disease, including depression, anxiety, or eating disorders.

4. Gregg Ten Elshof and Jackson Wu, *For Shame: Rediscovering the Virtues of a Maligned Emotion* (Grand Rapids, MI: Zondervan, 2021), 17.

5. Ten Elshof and Wu, *For Shame*, 17.

6. Dr. Hillary L. McBride, personal communication, May 26, 2020.

7. Brené Brown, *The Gifts of Imperfection: Let Go of Who You Think You're Supposed to Be and Embrace Who You Are* (Center City, MN: Hazelden, 2010), 39.

8. Timothy Keller, *Counterfeit Gods: The Empty Promises of Money, Sex, and Power, and the Only Hope That Matters* (New York: Dutton, 2009), 72–73.

9. Arnold Schwarzenegger and Peter Petre, *Total Recall: My Unbelievably True Life Story* (London: Simon & Schuster, 2013), 10.

10. Barack Obama, *A Promised Land* (New York: Crown, 2020), 71.

11. Saitō Tamaki, "Japan's 'Hikikomori' Population Could Top 10 Million," Nippon.com, Sept. 17, 2019, www.nippon.com/en/japan-topics/c05008/japan%E2%80%99s-hikikomori-population-could-top-10-million.html.

12. Roger Cohen, "Young Lives Interrupted," *New York Times*, November 2015, www.nytimes.com/2015/12/01/opinion/young -lives-interrupted.html.

13. Fyodor Dostoyevsky, *Crime and Punishment*, trans. David Magarshack (New York: Penguin Books, 1986), 34.

14. Thomas L. Friedman, *The World Is Flat: A Brief History of the Twenty-First Century* (New York: Farrar, Straus and Giroux, 2005), 400.

15. Similarly, a study examining profiles of ten prominent school shooters between 1996 and 1999 reported that "*in every case*, the shooters described how they had been ridiculed, taunted, teased, harassed, or bullied by peers (because of their inadequate appearance, social or athletic behavior), spurned by someone in whom they were romantically interested, or put down, in front of other students, by a teacher or school administrator, *all events that led to profound humiliation.*" See Brené Brown, *Atlas of the Heart: Mapping Meaningful Connection and the Language of Human Experience* (New York: Random House, 2021), 148.

16. I owe the expression "Swiss Cheese holes" to author Anne Lamott (source unknown).

Chapter 2: Covered by Grace

1. Thomas Merton, *New Seeds of Contemplation* (New York: New Directions, 1972), 36.

2. Lewis B. Smedes, *Shame and Grace: Healing the Shame We Don't Deserve* (Lexington: Lexington Accessible Textbook Service, 2006), 32.

3. Curt Thompson, *The Soul of Shame: Retelling the Stories We Believe about Ourselves* (Downers Grove, IL: InterVarsity Press, 2015), 99.

4. Merton, *New Seeds of Contemplation*, 34–35.

5. Merton, *New Seeds of Contemplation*, 34–35.

6. Merton, *New Seeds of Contemplation*, 34–35.

7. Merton, *New Seeds of Contemplation*, 34.

8. Shame is not hardwired into us, but children as young as fifteen months can learn to feel shame.

9. May Sarton, "Now I Become Myself," in *Collected Poems, 1930–1973* (New York: Norton, 1974), 156, used with permission. The poem was brought to my attention in Parker J. Palmer, *Let Your Life Speak: Listening for the Voice of Vocation* (San Francisco: Jossey-Bass, 2000), 9.

10. Richard Rohr, *The Wisdom Pattern: Order, Disorder, Reorder* (Cincinnati: Franciscan Media, 2021), 37.

11. Walter Brueggemann, *Genesis*, Interpretation (Atlanta: John Knox Press, 1982), 50.

12. Dr. Curt Thompson, personal conversation, June 11, 2020.

13. Kenneth E. Bailey, *Poet & Peasant* and *Through Peasant Eyes: A Literary-Cultural Approach to the Parables in Luke*, combined ed. (Grand Rapids: Eerdmans, 1983), 185–86.

Chapter 3: Encountering the Love of God

1. Bessel A. Van der Kolk, *The Body Keeps the Score: Brain, Mind, and Body in the Healing of Trauma* (New York: Penguin, 2015), 111–19.

2. Curt Thompson, *Anatomy of the Soul: Surprising Connections between Neuroscience and Spiritual Practices That Can Transform Your Life and Relationships* (Carol Stream, IL: Tyndale Refresh, 2010), 136–37.

3. The preceding examples are inspired by Thompson, *Anatomy of the Soul*.

4. For more on secure attachment, see also Susan M. Johnson, *Love Sense: The Revolutionary New Science of Romantic Relationships* (New York: Little, Brown, 2013).

5. Dr. Daniel Siegel describes the neural brain transformation his ninety-three-year-old patient experienced in Daniel J. Siegel, *Mindsight: The New Science of Personal Transformation* (New York: Bantam Books, 2011).

6. Thompson, *Anatomy of the Soul*, 137.

7. Seth Barnes, *The Art of Listening Prayer* (Gainsville, GA: Ashland Press, 2005), 23–24.

8. Ken Shigematsu, *Survival Guide for the Soul: How to Flourish Spiritually in a World That Pressures Us to Achieve* (Grand Rapids, MI: Zondervan, 2018), 75–86.

9. Thomas Keating, *Intimacy with God: An Introduction to Centering Prayer* (Chestnut Ridge, PA: Crossroad, 2009), 37–63.

10. Thomas Merton, *New Seeds of Contemplation* (New York: New Directions, 1972), 32.

11. Anthony de Mello, *The Song of the Bird* (Garden City, NY: Image Books, 1984), 63.

12. Thompson, *Anatomy of the Soul*, 143.

13. This is described in Deuteronomy 7:7 with the Hebrew word *hasaq*, which means binding love or love with desire.

14. Kazuo Ishiguro, *When We Were Orphans* (Toronto: Vintage Canada, 2001), 220.

15. Ephesians 3:19 (TPT) and Ephesians 1:18 (TPT) respectively.

Chapter 4: Seeing God's Face in Others

1. Proverbs 18:21 (ESV): "Death and life are in the power of the tongue, and those who love it will eat its fruits."

2. Daniel J. Siegel, *Mindsight: The New Science of Personal Transformation* (New York: Bantam Books, 2011), 152.

3. Robert Bly and William C. Booth, *A Little Book on the Human Shadow* (San Francisco: Harper & Row, 1988), 17–20.

4. John Bradshaw, *Healing the Shame That Binds You* (Deerfield Beach, FL: Health Communications, 2005), 174–76.

5. Bessel A. Van der Kolk, *The Body Keeps the Score: Brain, Mind, and Body in the Healing of Trauma* (New York: Penguin, 2015), 234.

6. Curt Thompson, *The Soul of Desire: Discovering the Neuroscience of Longing, Beauty, and Community* (Downers Grove, IL: InterVarsity Press, 2021), 144.

7. Jay Shetty, *Think Like a Monk: Train Your Mind for Peace and Purpose Every Day* (London: Thorsons, 2020), 162.

8. Brené Brown, *Daring Greatly: How the Courage to Be Vulnerable Transforms the Way We Live, Love, Parent, and Lead* (New York: Gotham Books, 2012), 82.

9. This is a video from Dan Siegel, "Dan Siegel: Name It to Tame It," YouTube, Dec. 8, 2014, www.youtube.com/watch?v=ZcDLz ppD4Jc&t=34s.

10. This thought came from Brené Brown, *I Thought It Was Just Me (But It Isn't): Women Reclaiming Power and Courage in a Culture of Shame* (New York: Gotham, 2007), 31–68.

11. Brown, *I Thought It Was Just Me (But It Isn't)*, 32.

12. Auburn Sandstrom, "One Phone Call Changed This Drug Addict's Life, and Her Story May Change Yours," *The Healthy* (blog), June 23, 2017, https://www.thehealthy.com/addiction /drugs-alcohol/drug-addiction-phone-call/.

Chapter 5: *Masterpiece in the Making*

1. Richard Rohr, "Original Shame and Original Blessing," Center for Action and Contemplation, July 1, 2016, https://cac.org/daily -meditations/original-shame-original-blessing-2016-07-01/.

2. The theologian Emil Brunner described our human condition as "magnificent ruin."

3. N. T. Wright makes this point in *After You Believe: Why Christian Character Matters* (New York: HarperCollins, 2012), 44–45.

4. Dr. N. T. Wright, personal communication, September 1, 2019.

5. Kelly McGonigal, *The Willpower Instinct: How Self-Control Works, Why It Matters, and What You Can Do to Get More of It* (New York: Avery, 2012), 176–89.

6. C. S. Lewis, *The Weight of Glory and Other Addresses* (San Francisco: HarperSanFrancisco, 2001), 45–46.

7. See, for example, N. T. Wright, *Surprised by Hope: Rethinking Heaven, the Resurrection, and the Mission of the Church: Six Sessions* (Grand Rapids, MI: Zondervan, 2010).

8. See Romans 8:1 and John 16:8.

9. Pamela Begeman, Mary Dwyer, Cherry Haisten, Gail

Fitzpatrick-Hopler, and Therese Saulnier, *The Welcoming Prayer: Consent on the Go, a 40-Day Praxis* (West Milford, NJ: Contemplative Outreach, 2018), 14.

10. Jay Shetty, *Think Like a Monk: Train Your Mind for Peace and Purpose Every Day* (London: Thorsons, 2020), 13.

11. Thomas R. Kelly, *A Testament of Devotion* (San Francisco: Harper SanFrancisco, 1996), 100.

12. James Finley, *Merton's Palace of Nowhere: A Search for God through Awareness of the True Self* (Notre Dame, IN: Ave Maria Press, 1978, 2003), 114.

13. Daniel J. Siegel, *Becoming Aware: A 21-Day Mindfulness Program for Reducing Anxiety and Cultivating Calm* (New York: TarcherPerigee, 2021), 17.

14. David G. Benner, *Surrender to Love: Discovering the Heart of Christian Spirituality* (Downers Grove, IL: InterVarsity Press, 2003), 80–81.

Chapter 6: Overcoming Envy

1. Cameron Russell, "Looks Aren't Everything. Believe Me, I'm a Model," https://www.ted.com/talks/cameron_russell_looks_aren_t_everything_believe_me_i_m_a_model?Language=en).

2. "Why No One Feels Rich: The Psychology of Inequality," npr.org, April 22, 2019, www.npr.org/transcripts/715145723.

3. Yuval Noah Harari, *Sapiens: A Brief History of Humankind* (Toronto: McClelland & Stewart, 2014), 384.

4. Jon Tyson, *The Burden Is Light: Liberating Your Life from the Tyranny of Performance and Success* (Colorado Springs: Multnomah, 2018), 21.

5. "Why No One Feels Rich."

6. See, for example, Greg Lukianoff and Jonathan Haidt, *The Coddling of the American Mind: How Good Intentions and Bad Ideas Are Setting Up a Generation for Failure* (New York: Penguin, 2019). See also Jonathan Haidt, "The Dangerous Experiment on Teen Girls," *The Atlantic*, November 21, 2021, https://www.theatlantic

.com/ideas/archive/2021/11/facebooks-dangerous-experiment-teen-girls/620767/.

7. David Brooks, *The Road to Character* (New York: Random House, 2015), 227.

8. Dietrich Bonhoeffer, *Life Together: A Discussion of Christian Fellowship* (San Francisco: HarperSanFrancisco, 1978), 86.

9. Jay Shetty, *Think Like a Monk: Train Your Mind for Peace and Purpose Every Day* (London: Thorsons, 2020), 207.

10. "Reimagining the Examen" is a free app that plays a little music and then guides you into the Examen.

11. Anthony de Mello is quoted in Alberto Ribera, *The 7 Moments of Coaching: Stories of Inner Journeys* (Barcelona: Reverte Management, 2021), 73.

12. Caroline Leaf, *Switch on Your Brain: The Key to Peak Happiness, Thinking, and Health* (Grand Rapids, MI: Baker, 2015), 66.

Chapter 7: Embracing Our Limits

1. Carol S. Dweck, *Mindset: The New Psychology of Success* (New York: Ballantine Books, 2008).

2. Christopher Marlowe, *Doctor Faustus* (London: W. Oxberry, 1818), 4.

3. Marlowe, *Doctor Faustus*, 17.

4. Greg McKeown, *Essentialism: The Disciplined Pursuit of Less* (New York: Currency, 2014), 169.

5. Wendell Berry, "Faustian Economics," *Harper's Magazine*, May 2008, 35–42.

6. I am drawing on the insights of Stephen A. Seamands, *Ministry in the Image of God: The Trinitarian Shape of Christian Service* (Downers Grove, IL: InterVarsity Press, 2005), 23–26.

7. Parker J. Palmer, *Let Your Life Speak: Listening for the Voice of Vocation* (San Francisco: Jossey-Bass, 2000), 47.

8. Palmer, *Let Your Life Speak*, 47.

9. Thomas Merton, *New Seeds of Contemplation* (New York: New Directions, 1972), 45.

10. Palmer, *Let Your Life Speak*, 49.

11. Gabor Maté, *When the Body Says No: The Cost of Hidden Stress* (Toronto: Vintage Canada, 2003), 257.

12. James Martin, *The Jesuit Guide to (Almost) Everything: A Spirituality for Real Life* (New York: HarperCollins, 2010), 316.

13. Martin, *The Jesuit Guide to (Almost) Everything*, 324–25.

14. Gordon T. Smith, *Your Calling Here and Now: Making Sense of Vocation* (Downers Grove, IL: InterVarsity Press, 2022), 53.

15. Thomas Merton, *Love and Living* (Orlando: Harcourt, 1979), 11–12, quoted in Richard Rohr, *Immortal Diamond: The Search for Our True Self* (San Francisco: Jossey-Bass, 2013).

16. McKeown, *Essentialism*, 165. See also Clayton M. Christensen, James Allworth, and Karen Dillon, *How Will You Measure Your Life?* (New York: Harper Business, 2012), 80–82.

17. Julie Canlis, *A Theology of the Ordinary* (Wenatchee, WA: Godspeed Press, 2017), 16–18.

18. To learn more about Dave Hataj's journey, see Dave Hataj, *Good Work: How Blue Collar Business Can Change Lives, Communities, and the World* (Chicago: Moody Publishers, 2020).

19. "Overcoming the Need to Be Exceptional," The School of Life, May 15, 2019, https://www.theschooloflife.com/thebookoflife/overcoming-the-need-to-be-exceptional/.

20. Licia Corbella, "Corbella: Retirement for Pastor Ray Matheson Means Not Much Has Changed," *Calgary Herald*, September 26, 2020, https://calgaryherald.com/news/local-news/corbella-retirement-for-pastor-ray-matheson-means-not-much-has-changed.

21. Henri J. M. Nouwen, *The Return of the Prodigal Son: A Story of Homecoming* (New York: Image, 1993), 120–21. Henri Nouwen is also cited in Peter Scazzero and Warren Bird, *The Emotionally Healthy Church: A Strategy for Discipleship That Actually Changes Lives* (Grand Rapids, MI: Zondervan, 2003), 144–45.

22. I have adapted this prayer from Mary Mrozowski and Cindy

Bunch, *Be Kind to Yourself* (Downers Grove, IL: InterVarsity Press, 2020), 91.

Chapter 8: Fulfilling Our Potential

1. Desmond Tutu, *God Has a Dream: A Vision of Hope for Our Time* (New York: Doubleday, 2005), 86.
2. Curt Thompson, *The Soul of Shame: Retelling the Stories We Believe about Ourselves* (Downers Grove, IL: InterVarsity Press, 2015), 99.
3. C. S. Lewis, quoted in Thompson, *The Soul of Shame*, 99.
4. Henri J. M Nouwen, *Here and Now: Living in the Spirit* (New York: Crossroad, 1994), 98–99.
5. Summer Allen, "The Science of Generosity," Greater Good Science Center at UC Berkeley, May 2018, https://ggsc.berkeley.edu/images/uploads/GGSC-JTF_White_Paper-Generosity-FINAL.pdf., 3.
6. Allen, "The Science of Generosity," 23.
7. His Holiness the Dalai Lama and Archbishop Desmond Tutu, with Douglas Abrams, *The Book of Joy: Lasting Happiness in a Changing World* (New York: Viking, 2016), 265–66.

Chapter 9: Awakening to Beauty

1. Dr. Curt Thompson, personal conversation, June 11, 2020.
2. Kelly McGonigal, *The Joy of Movement: How Exercise Helps Us Find Happiness, Hope, Connection, and Courage* (New York: Avery, 2019), 160.
3. Simone Weil, *Waiting for God* (San Francisco: Harper Perennial Modern Classics, 2009), 100.
4. Weil, *Waiting for God*, 104.
5. Andrew B. Newberg and Mark Robert Waldman, *How God Changes Your Brain: Breakthrough Findings from a Leading Neuroscientist* (New York: Ballantine, 2010), 110.
6. Newberg and Waldman, *How God Changes Your Brain*, 109.
7. Elaine Scarry, *On Beauty and Being Just* (Princeton, NJ: Princeton University Press, 2010), 88.

8. Adam Hoffman, "How Awe Makes Us Generous," Greater Good, August 3, 2015, https://greatergood.berkeley.edu/article/item /how_awe_makes_us_generous.

9. Bobby Scobey, "In Bill Moyers' Book *A World of Ideas II*, Jacob Needleman Remembers," Sermon Central, March 20, 2007, www .sermoncentral.com/sermon-illustrations/31834/in-bill-moyers -s-book-a-world-of-ideas-ii-jacob-by-bobby-scobey.

10. Abraham Goldberg, Kevin M. Leyden, and Thomas J. Scotto, "Untangling What Makes Cities Livable: Happiness in Five Cities," ResearchGate, Sept. 2012, www.researchgate.net/publication /224525238_Untangling_What_Makes_Cities_Livable _Happiness_in_Five_Cities. See also Cody C. Delistraty, "The Beauty-Happiness Connection: Looking at Lovely Things—and People—Can Improve Quality of Life," *The Atlantic*, Aug. 15, 2014, www.theatlantic.com/health/archive/2014/08/the-beauty happiness-connection/375678/.

11. Curt Thompson, *The Soul of Desire: Discovering the Neuroscience of Longing, Beauty, and Community* (Downers Grove, IL: InterVarsity Press, 2021), 6.

Chapter 10: Choosing Joy

1. Martin Sheen, "Spirituality of Imagination," On Being with Krista Tippett, June 22, 2017, https://onbeing.org/programs/martin -sheen-spirituality-of-imagination-jun2017/.

2. Hillary L. McBride, *The Wisdom of Your Body: Finding Healing, Wholeness, and Connection through Embodied Living* (Toronto: Collins, 2021), 110.

3. Shawn Achor, *The Happiness Advantage: The Seven Principles That Fuel Success and Performance at Work* (London: Virgin, 2011), 175.

4. Rick Hanson, *Hardwiring Happiness: The New Brain Science of Contentment, Calm, and Confidence* (New York: Harmony Books, 2013). See also Kathleen Toohill, "What Negative Thinking Does to Your Brain," July 31, 2015, https://archive.attn.com/stories /2587/what-negative-thinking-does-your-brain.

5. Robert A. Emmons, *Thanks!: How Practicing Gratitude Can Make You Happier* (New York: Houghton Mifflin, 2008), 3.

6. David Steindl-Rast is referenced in His Holiness the Dalai Lama and Archbishop Desmond Tutu, with Douglas Abrams, *The Book of Joy: Lasting Happiness in a Changing World* (New York: Viking, 2016), 246.

7. C. S. Lewis and Peter Kreeft, *The Shadow-Lands of C. S. Lewis: The Man behind the Movie* (San Francisco: Ignatius Press, 1994), 47. In Lewis' *Surprised by Joy,* he contends that unsatisfied desire is greater than any satisfaction. C. S. Lewis, *Surprised by Joy: The Shape of My Early Life* (New York: Harcourt, Brace & World, 1984), 18.

8. Fyodor Dostoyevsky, *The Brothers Karamazov,* trans. David Magarshack (Harmondsworth: Penguin, 1982), 275.

9. Kelly McGonigal, *The Joy of Movement: How Exercise Helps Us Find Happiness, Hope, Connection, and Courage* (New York: Avery, 2019), 137.

10. St. Ignatius of Loyola, *The Autobiography of St. Ignatius of Loyola,* ed. J.F.X. O'Connor, S.J. (New York: Benziger Brothers, 1900), 20–22.

11. See Ecclesiastes 2:24; 11:9; see also Choon-Leong Seow, ed., *Ecclesiastes: A New Translation with Introduction and Commentary,* The Anchor Yale Bible Commentaries (New Haven: Yale University Press, 2008), 1.

12. C. S. Lewis, *The Screwtape Letters* (New York: Macmillan, 1982), 101.

13. Mark Buchanan, *The Rest of God: Restoring Your Soul by Restoring Sabbath* (Nashville: W Publishing Group, 2006), 126–27.

14. Abraham Joshua Heschel, *The Sabbath: Its Meaning for Modern Man* (New York: Farrar, Straus and Young, 1951), 15.

15. Daniel Kahneman, *Thinking, Fast and Slow* (Toronto: Anchor Canada, 2013), 386.

16. His Holiness the Dalai Lama and Archbishop Desmond Tutu, with Douglas Abrams, *The Book of Joy* (New York: Viking, 2016),

244–46. See also Anthony Ray Hinton, Lara Love Hardin, and Bryan Stevenson, *The Sun Does Shine: How I Found Life and Freedom on Death Row* (New York: St. Martin's Press, 2018).

17. I am drawing from Alain de Botton's insights. See the article, "A Better Word Than Happiness," The School of Life, www.the schooloflife.com/thebookoflife/a-better-word-than-happiness -eudaimonia/.

18. Maisie Ward, *Return to Chesterton* (London: Sheed & Ward, 1952), 137.

19. Elisabeth Kübler-Ross, *Death: The Final Stage of Growth* (New York: Touchstone, 1986), 93.

Epilogue: Nothing Wasted

1. Rick Hanson, *Hardwiring Happiness: The New Brain Science of Contentment, Calm, and Confidence* (New York: Harmony Books, 2013), 131–46.

2. Curt Thompson, *The Soul of Desire: Discovering the Neuroscience of Longing, Beauty, and Community* (Downers Grove, IL: InterVarsity Press, 2021), 156–68.